comforts of home

comforts of home
simple knitted accents

e rika **k** night

PHOTOGRAPHY BY JOHN HESELTINE

Martingale
& COMPANY

This book is dedicated to generation Y2K,

hopefully to inspire a little homespun creativity

in a high-tech world!

Martingale & Company
PO Box 118
Bothell, WA 98041-0118
www.patchwork.com

Fiber Studio Press is an imprint of Martingale & Company.

Originated by Classic Scan Ltd, Singapore.
Printed in China by Toppan Pinting Company.
05 04 03 02 01 00   6 5 4 3 2 1

Library of Congress Cataloging-in-Publication Data is available.

A BERRY BOOK
Conceived, edited and designed by Susan Berry, in association
with Debbie Mole and Erika Knight, for Collins & Brown
Design and Art Direction: Debbie Mole
Editor: Sally Harding

MISSION STATEMENT
We are dedicated to providing quality
products and service by working
together to inspire creativity and to
enrich the lives we touch.

contents listing

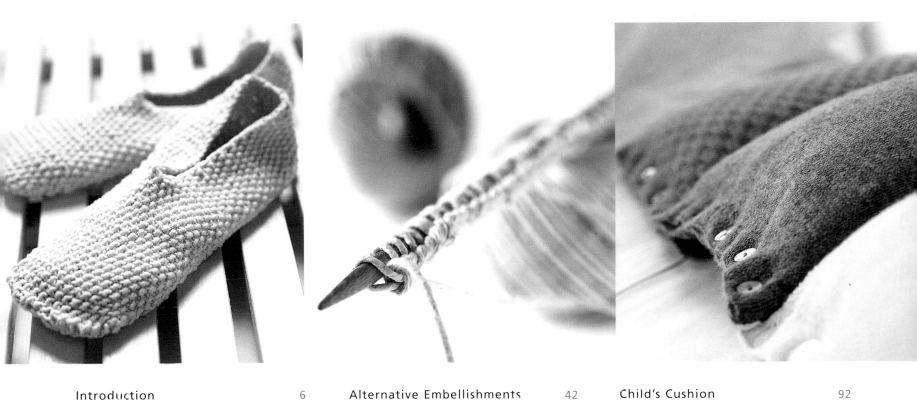

knitting is simple

Take two smooth wooden sticks and a continuous length of "yarn," and in four simple steps ~ **in, over, under, off** ~ make a **stitch.** Make several stitches to make a **row.** Make several rows to make a **fabric.** This books aims to **take the pain out of knitting.** Forget complex knitting patterns. Here we go, **back to the very basics** with **simple language · no abbreviations · no difficult shaping · no charts or diagrams to follow · no stitch gauge rules.** Knitted pieces **based on simple rectangles** are **easy to knit, speedy to knit.** To begin, just learn to cast on, knit two basic stitches, and bind off. It is all you need to know. Simple stitches in simple shapes and simple yarns create beautiful pieces for every day of your life and **for every room in your home** ~ for living · for sleeping · for bathing.

For sheer pleasure, I like to use **bamboo knitting needles** ~ light, sleek, and smooth. They are beautiful to look at and beautiful to the touch, and they allow the knitting to slide. Experiment with the feel of natural materials from string to cashmere. Try them all ~ wool, cotton, linen, sisal, mohair, chenille. **"Feel" the different textures.** Then add to the fun by experimenting with **non-traditional materials** ~ wire, nylon, twine, rags, cloth tapes, and raffia. Knitting creates a **back-to-basics aesthetic.** It is a **nurturing craft** and an honest one. Today, giving something handmade and personalized is both a caring act and **the ultimate in luxury and chic.** Just get going, break the rules. Take pleasure using texture and creating something by hand that is **simple, beautiful, and easy.**

enjoy

yarns: natural wood

NATURAL WOOD TONES: For inspiration for color in your knitting, look to natural, hard materials such as wood, stone, slate, steel, and glass. They each have their own inherent palette of hues, which comfortably contrast and coexist with softer cotton, linen, wool, leather, suede, and textiles to create a home rich in surface textures. The timeless neutrals provided by these rich natural elements are highlighted by earth and vegetable tones, as well as indigos and whites. On this and the following pages I explore some

1: Parcel string Simple, basic, functional, and inexpensive, parcel string is also rich in tone , and texture.

2: Sisal string Coarse and naturally abrasive, sisal adds authenticity to simple pieces or details.

3 & 4: Cotton yarns Naturally dry and soft,

cotton yarns are available in a wide variety of tones and textures. Fine cotton is beautifully refined when worked in simple textures like seed stitch.

5: Garden twines Like sisal, garden twine is rough and rustic, but more pliable.

of these combinations as sources for selecting yarns for simple, beautiful projects for the home.

Natural wood is a good starting point for design ideas. From worn bark, to weathered surfaces, smoothly polished cork and honey-colored floors, wood is rich in warm color and tone. Wood, rough or smooth, is naturally complemented by the simple textures of coarse yellow sisal string, fine ivory-colored parcel string, rough garden twine, smooth classic ecru cotton yarns, and grainy buttons.

yarns : stone & steel

1: Alpaca Soft, warm alpaca is rich in natural tones.

2: Mélange yarns Contrasting strands twisted together form unique yarn mixtures.

3: Leather string Matte, smooth leather string complements the stone and steel theme.

4: Chenille A velvet-textured cotton.

5: Felted yarn Light, voluminous lofty wool.

6: Bouclé An airy, lightweight looped or curled woollen yarn.

7: Synthetic fibers Transparent, pearlized man-made threads add surface contrast.

STONE & STEEL TONES: Like natural wood, stone and steel is a fertile source of color inspiration. Here shades of stone, pebble, and pearl are balanced with natural shadows of steel, slate, and carbon.

Matte, smooth, grainy, or polished, absolute neutrals—tone on tone—create a classic elegant modern interior. For this theme, soft alpaca in subtle natural tones, yarns with mélanges of tone and texture, luxurious quick-to-knit felted wool, and curly textured bouclé create voluminous, lofty, and weightless fabrics. To counter and complement this, smooth leather, velvety chenille, and pearlized transparent nylons add a unique harder edge to a simple contemporary look. Consider authentic troche pearl buttons for finishing touches; they reflect the subtle tints and hues of grays, making them a natural choice where quality is not compromised.

yarns : soft suede

SOFT SUEDE TONES: The themes of soft suede and smooth leather are good illustrations of how simple textural differences alter our view of color. Texture can soften or sharpen by its depths of shadows or strength of hightlights. Suede here inspires softly blurred textures that add an elegantly plump yet comfortable "Sunday"

1: Merino Soft, light, and airy wool yarn.

2: Bouclé Curly yarn effective for simple cushions and throws.

3: Chenille Velvety cotton, luxurious in both fine and fat weights.

4: Angora Ultra fine, extremely soft yarn from the angora rabbit.

5: Cashmere A yarn that is the ultimate natural classic luxury.

feeling to any living space—yarns that feel as beautiful as they look and that are warm and sensual to the touch. Smooth, rounded merino wool and precious and intimate blends of angora, alpaca, cashmere, and mohair create downy suede surfaces in a delicate, sophisticated palette of biscuit, blonde, palomino, and butter.

yarns : leather

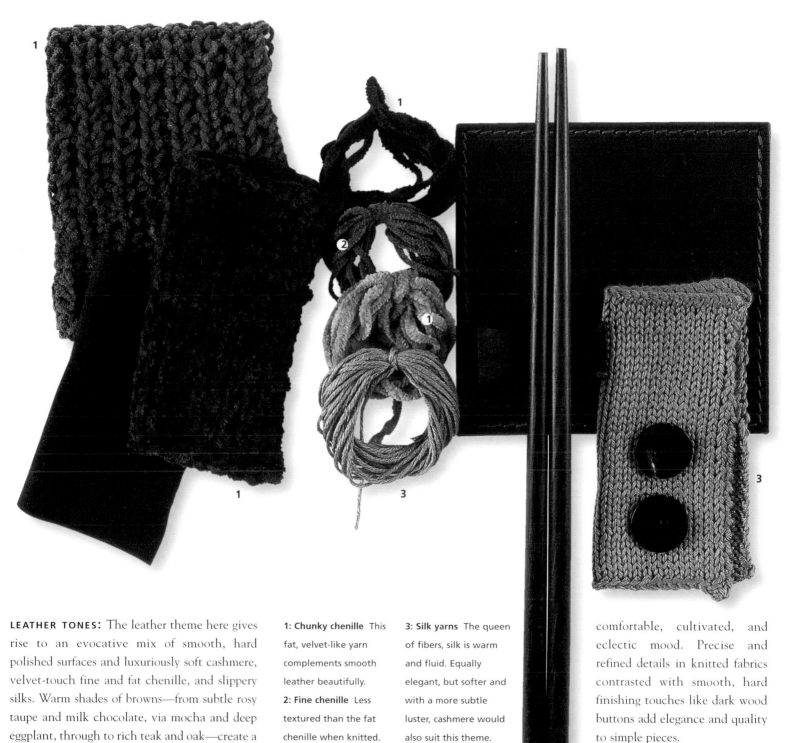

LEATHER TONES: The leather theme here gives rise to an evocative mix of smooth, hard polished surfaces and luxuriously soft cashmere, velvet-touch fine and fat chenille, and slippery silks. Warm shades of browns—from subtle rosy taupe and milk chocolate, via mocha and deep eggplant, through to rich teak and oak—create a

1: Chunky chenille This fat, velvet-like yarn complements smooth leather beautifully.

2: Fine chenille Less textured than the fat chenille when knitted.

3: Silk yarns The queen of fibers, silk is warm and fluid. Equally elegant, but softer and with a more subtle luster, cashmere would also suit this theme.

comfortable, cultivated, and eclectic mood. Precise and refined details in knitted fabrics contrasted with smooth, hard finishing touches like dark wood buttons add elegance and quality to simple pieces.

yarns:earth

EARTH TONES: Natural earth tones inspire a new look at neutrals. Add living warmth to surface and texture in the home with a rhythmic mix of vigorous greens—algae, lichen, and moss—and earthy taupe and peat. Rustic tweed-effect yarns and bulky tweeds, coordinate with cotton, chenille, silk, and natural linen for a rich

1: Chenille Velvety chenille blends well with the organic theme.

2: Cotton Smooth or rustic, fat or fine.

3: Silk Delicate, smooth, satiny fiber.

4: Tweed Provides instant texture through mixed color.

5: Ridge textures Purl-stitch ridges add texture.

6: Linen A cool, dry ancient rustic yarn.

depth of color and a sense of warmth and protection. This look can be further enhanced with "rough" reverse-stockinette-stitch and purl-stitch ridges, and detailed with authentic horn buttons. Earth tone and texture combinations are unexpectedly modern in their application for home decoration.

yarns : vegetable

VEGETABLE TONES: The absolute classic and timeless neutrals shown on the previous pages are highlighted by seasonal earth hues as well as by these vegetable tones. Derived from the primal essential ingredients for everyday living, vegetable colors provide creative sustenance for the seasonal home. Fresh fleshy figs, tender pink

1: Merino and cotton mix Mixing cotton and wool in a yarn creates an ideal smoothness and elasticity.
2: Chunky chenille Soft, velvety chenille comes in a range of vegetable tones.
3: Fine chenille Thinner weights of chenille produce smoother knitted fabrics than the thicker ones.

shoots of aromatic basil, pale leafy ribs of celery, mauvy tips of young asparagus prove how often intense tones of color easily coexist in nature. Velvety chenille, both fine and fat, and mixed yarn made from soft merino wool and cotton fibers supply the vegetable shades that bring life to this design story.

yarns : indigo & denim

INDIGO AND DENIM TONES: Casual, easy, and relaxed, tones of indigo, denim, and chambray are modern "neutrals" for any room in the home. Indigo is an ancient natural dye that has been used to color cotton for thousands of years.

The popularity of indigo is based on its extraordinary quality to fade gradually and age naturally and beautifully with wear. In its many permutations, indigo is evocative of sun-bleached beaches and the seashore—a mood you

1: Mid-blue denim yarn The traditional unwashed mid-blue denim hue.

2: Stone-washed denim yarn The shade of gracefully faded indigo.

3: Dark blue denim yarn A deep, dark indigo tone.

4: Off-white denim yarn Stone, off-white, and ecru shades provide contrast to the blues.

5: Chenille A soft complement for cool, smooth cotton yarns.

6: Cotton yarn Matte or shiny cottons fit perfectly into the denim look.

can take into your interiors by making cushions and throws with denim knitting yarn. This yarn is 100 percent cotton and knits into a slightly firmer, weightier fabric than other cotton yarns. Denim yarns in shades of indigo offset with basic natural tones of ecru and stone create casual classic designs.

Both velvety chenille and smooth and matte cotton yarns in cool blues and warmer off-whites will enhance the overall indigo theme.

yarns : white

1: Merino This soft wool yarn is good for refined knitted detail.

2: Merino and cotton mix A mixed merino wool and cotton yarn, extra soft, yet cool.

3: Raffia Raffia cast-on and bound-off edges add a modern texture.

4: Cord Use to trim or accessorise knits.

5: Rag knit Strips of terry, muslin, and net, and lengths of raffia, bouclé, chenille, and cord all knitted together.

6: Fine cotton Smooth cotton yarns accentuate stitch patterns.

WHITE: Absolutely essential to any home are whites. Implacable, indispensable, fresh, clean, and calming, they ground the neutral palette. White is the color of total order, yet it is rich in diversity of texture and tone—frosty textures of glass and ice, transluscent mother-of-pearl, chalky soft chenille, fine piqué cottons, whisper-light wool, milky white muslin, opaque nylon, and papery raffia. Textured whites translate into the finest or coarsest of knits.

equipment

TOOLS & MATERIALS: The equipment required to make any of the projects in this book is simple, inexpensive, and readily available. Here are some of the basics to start you off.

yarn: First, you will need knitting yarn. You do not have to restrict yourself to the conventional either! There are many materials that, although they are not usually used for knitting, will do just as well. For example, string, cloth tape, wire, felt, ribbon, twine—in fact, you can knit practically anything you want that is flexible enough.

knitting needles: These are available in a variety of sizes from fine to fat. My favorite type are bamboo, which are beautiful to work with as they are light and smooth and allow the knitting to slide. They also look great reclining on your couch or throw, or embedded in some wonderful textile, should a friend drop in unexpectedly.

tape measure or ruler: You'll need this for measuring knitting as you proceed.

scissors: For cutting yarn or loose ends on knitting, a sharp pair of scissors is a must.

glass-headed pins: Pins with glass heads are easy to spot when sewing up your knitting— you'll be sure not to leave any behind.

sewing needle: Use large blunt-ended needles to sew your knitting together with yarn.

buttons: When projects are so simple, the detailing is crucial. Buttons are perfect for use as simple but effective highlights, so keep them in mind and choose them carefully when finishing off your knitting.

cork: A wine cork is handy for sticking knitting needle tips into, to prevent stitches from falling off, and to prevent sharp points from poking through if you travel with your knitting like I do.

bag: Lastly, find a suitable bag for keeping knitting clean and carrying it with you.

techniques

GAUGE: There is no mystery in "stitch gauge." Put very simply, by changing the size of your knitting needles, you can control the size of your knitting. As a basic rule *fine needles go with fine yarn and fat needles with fat yarn.* You can see here the difference in size of the stitches when this rule is applied (see right). The secret to getting the best from any yarn is to experiment to discover the best size needle to use with a particular yarn. You could knit up several yarns in an evening to find out how easily they knit and the look and feel of the fabric you prefer. The same yarn knitted

fine yarn: fine needles

medium yarn: medium needles

fat yarn: fat needles

medium yarn: fine needles

medium yarn: medium needles

medium yarn: fat needles

on different-size needles looks quite different—from very dense to very loose (see left).

If you know the size of each stitch (see page 124), you can make a piece of knitting any width you want, but for most of the simple projects in the following chapters exact size is not important—relax, a few too many or too few stitches will not make much difference. Enjoy the process of knitting and the texture—remember, yarns have different qualities, and by using fatter or finer knitting needles you can achieve a fabric that you are happy with.

one : loop
Loop the yarn over your left thumb with the ball end on the left and a long end on the right.

four : down
Pull the yarn on the needle down through the loop on your thumb to make the first loop.

CASTING ON: Before you can start knitting, the first thing to do is to "cast on." This is the process of making loops or "stitches" with a length of yarn on one of the knitting needles. Simple! There are many methods for doing this, but one of the easiest is shown here. (See page 30 for how to make a "knit" cast on at the beginning of a row.) If you haven't tried casting on before, take a little time to practice and it will become automatic after a while. When you start a knitting pattern it will tell you exactly how many stitches to cast on before you begin.

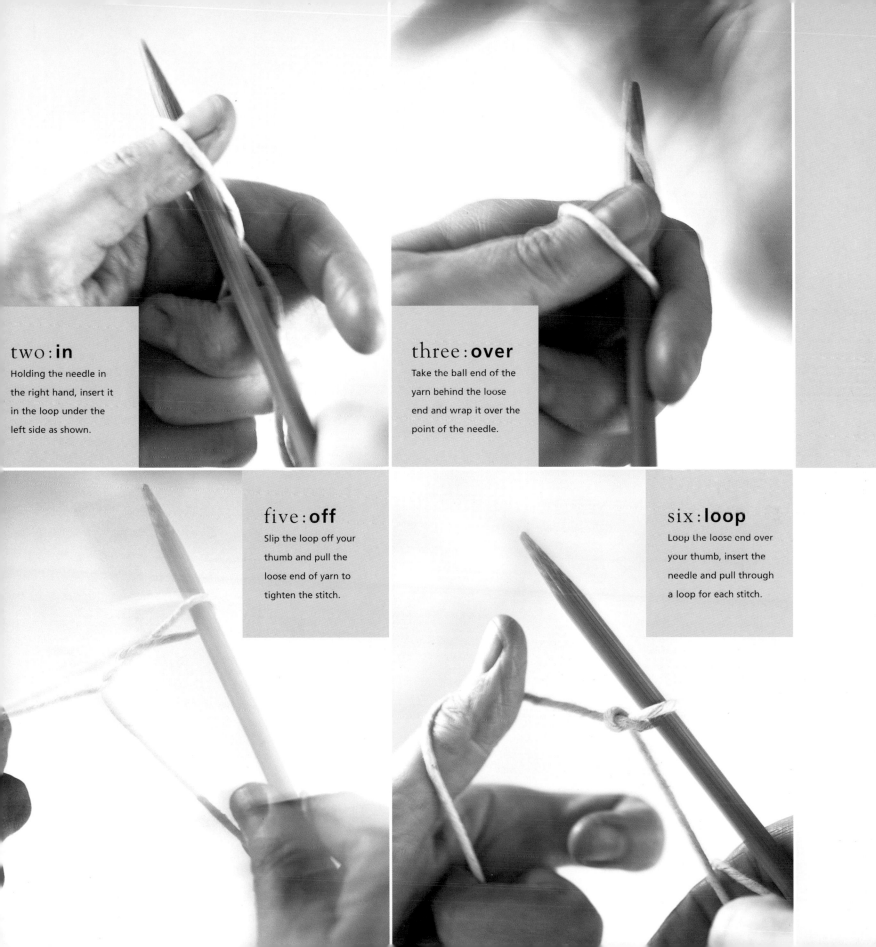

two : **in**

Holding the needle in the right hand, insert it in the loop under the left side as shown.

three : **over**

Take the ball end of the yarn behind the loose end and wrap it over the point of the needle.

five : **off**

Slip the loop off your thumb and pull the loose end of yarn to tighten the stitch.

six : **loop**

Loop the loose end over your thumb, insert the needle and pull through a loop for each stitch.

one : **knit 2**

To begin binding off, first knit 2 stitches so that there are 2 loops on the right-hand needle.

four : **off**

Let first stitch drop off the right-hand needle, so only the second stitch remains on it.

BINDING OFF: To finish your piece of knitted fabric so that it will not unravel, you "bind off" the stitches. This is the process of drawing one stitch loop through the next all along the needle as you knit across a row. When the instructions just say "bind off" it means to knit each stitch as you bind off. But sometimes it will tell you to "bind off in pattern," in which case you should knit or purl each stitch in the pattern you were using in the previous rows, as you bind off. Binding off a few stitches within the knitted fabric (and casting on again in the next row to replace the stitches) is also used for buttonholes.

two : **in**

Insert the point of the left-hand needle in the first stitch on the right-hand needle as shown.

three : **over**

Lift the first stitch on the right-hand needle over the second stitch on the right-hand needle.

five : **repeat**

Repeat across the row, knitting next stitch and lifting first stitch over it, until one stitch remains.

six : **finish**

To finish the bind off, cut working yarn, pull the end through the last loop and tighten.

one : **in**

Insert point of right-hand needle in first stitch on left-hand needle as shown.

MAKING A KNIT STITCH: After casting on the appropriate number of stitches as shown on pages 22 and 23, you can begin your first row of knitting. The knit stitch is made in a simple four-step process as shown here, repeating the steps until all the stitches on the left-hand needle have been transferred to the right-hand needle. Once you have completed the row, transfer the needle holding the worked stitches to your left hand, and begin again with another row of knit stitches, to create a fabric known as garter stitch (shown in close up).

two : **over**

Holding the yarn in the right hand, wrap it over point of right-hand needle to make a loop.

three : under

Pull the new loop on right-hand needle under and through first loop on the left-hand needle.

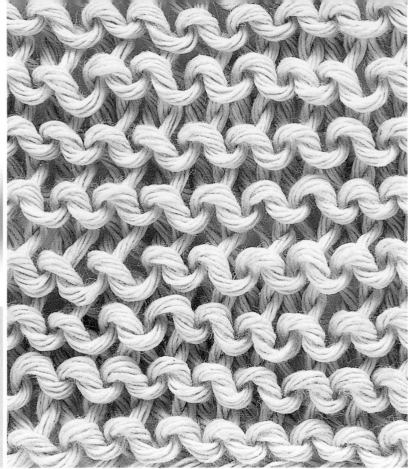

four : off

Slide stitch off the point of left-hand needle. You have now knitted one stitch onto right needle.

one : **in**
Insert point of right-hand needle in first stitch on left-hand needle as shown.

MAKING A PURL STITCH: The purl stitch is worked in much the same way as the knit stitch, but the yarn is held at the front of the work instead of the back. Knit and purl is all there is to know! Combining these two is the basis of all knitted fabric. Stockinette stitch is made by working one row knit and one purl alternately: the right side (or knit side) is smooth and the wrong side (purl) is ridged or rough. When the purl side is the right side, the fabric is called reverse stockinette stitch. Other knitted textures are made by using knit and purl stitches in the same row.

two : **over**
Holding the yarn in the right hand, wrap yarn over point of right-hand needle to make a loop.

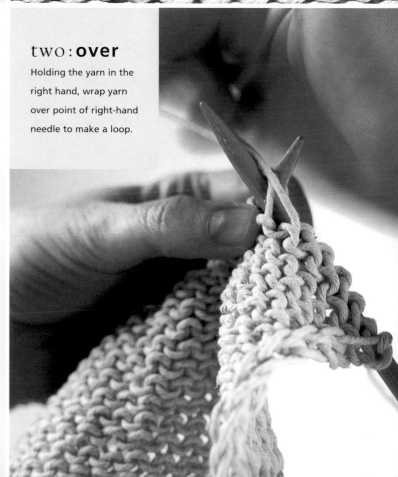

three : under

Pull the new loop on right-hand needle under and through first loop on the left-hand needle.

four : off

Slide stitch off the point of left-hand needle, leaving new purled stitch on right needle.

one : **in**

To increase by "casting on," insert right-hand needle in first stitch and pull a loop through.

two : **in**

Do not drop stitch from left needle. Insert left needle in new loop and slip it off right needle.

three : **on**

You now have an extra stitch on the left-hand needle. Begin the next row in the usual way.

INCREASING: Adding or taking away stitches from a row will shape your knitting. These techniques are called "increasing" and "decreasing" and are used to shape the slippers on page 96. One of the simplest ways of adding stitches is to "cast on" new loops at the end of a row in the same way you do when starting to knit (see page 22) or to work a "knit" cast on at the beginning of a row as shown here. An equally simple increase technique is to knit into the front, then back of the same stitch before slipping it off the left-hand needle—making two from one.

one:**in**

Insert right-hand needle in two stitches (through front or back loops) and wrap yarn over needle.

two:**under**

With two stitches still on left-hand needle, pull yarn under and through both stitches at once.

three:**off**

Drop two stitches from left-hand needle. You have just made two stitches into one.

DECREASING: One way to reduce the number of stitches in a row is to "bind off" stitches in the same way you finish off a row of knitting (see page 24). This creates a little ledge on the edge of the knitting, so if you only want to decrease one stitch at the side of your knitting and make a smooth slant, a better and simpler method is to knit (or purl) two stitches together. This is done by inserting the right-hand needle through two stitches on the left-hand needle at the same time (either through the front or back of the loops) and knitting them both off at once.

living

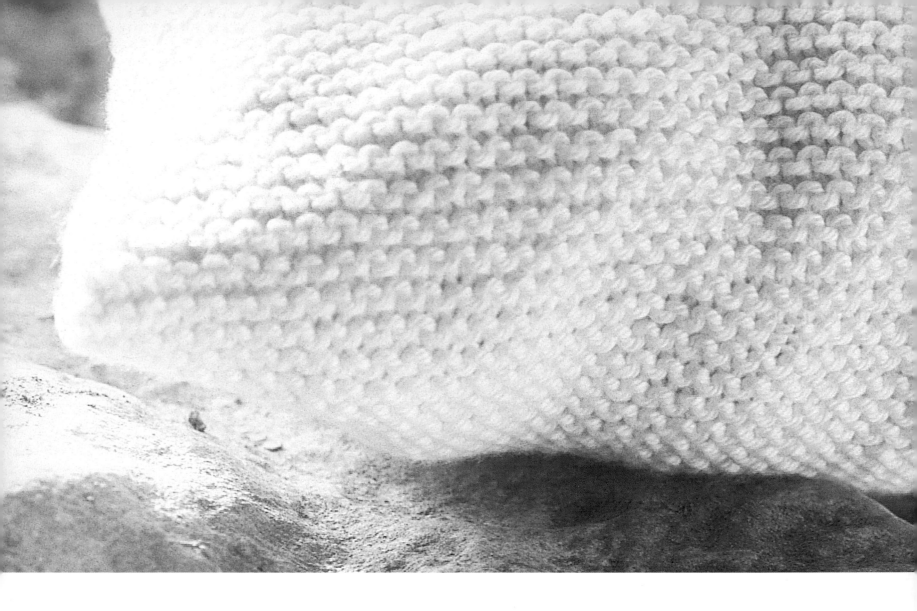

simple cushions : cotton or chenille

Knitted in cotton or chenille yarn in garter stitch, this cushion has a beautiful raised texture. No increasing, difficult shaping, or tricky finishing details are needed. Its simplicity is its major design feature: it is a straight length of knitting, folded twice, and then simply seamed together. This clean-cut style allows the yarn qualities to shine, so varying the kind of yarn has a big effect on its look and feel. Chenille gives a much softer, more luxurious finish to the cushion than the natural, cool

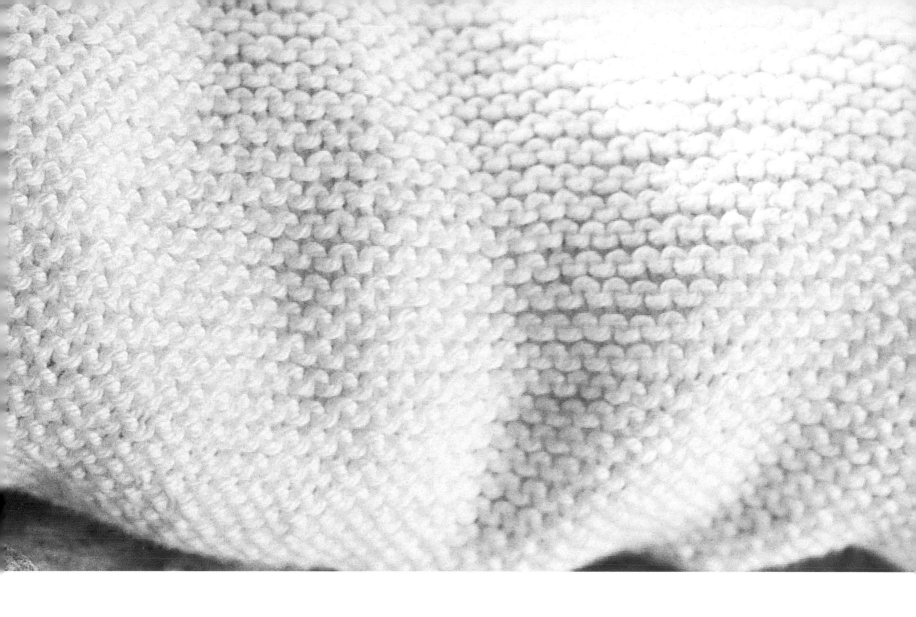

cotton. You could also try working it in ultra-tactile yarns like alpaca or cashmere. Or use a soft string

for a more contemporary, crisper finish. Neutral colors—cream, ecru, beige, and off-white—serve to

emphasize the textural resonances of the yarn. Several cushions in toning shades will complement

each other. The cushion here measures 19$\frac{3}{4}$" square, but you can create whatever size cushion you

like by following the simple calculation guide on page 124.

how to make : simple cushions

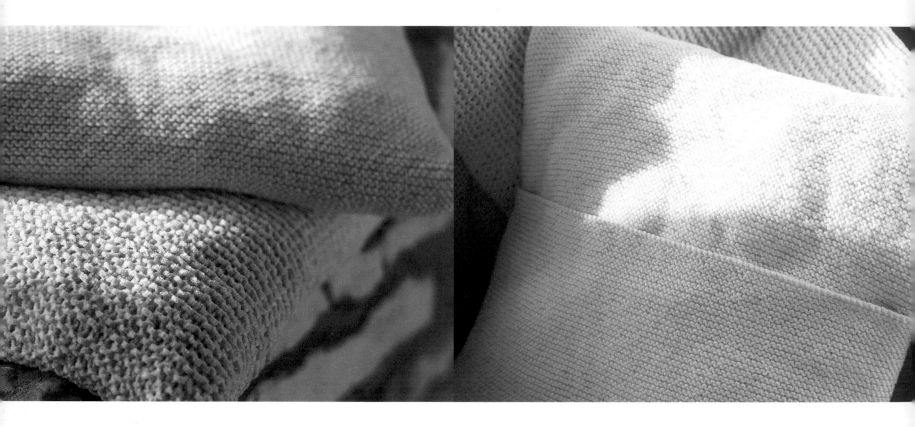

FOR THE SIMPLE COTTON CUSHION: Use 10 x 1³/₄oz balls Rowan *Handknit D.K. Cotton*, pair size 6 needles, sewing needle and pins, 19³/₄"-square feather pillow form

METHOD FOR THE SIMPLE COTTON CUSHION (*worked in one piece*)**:** Using size 6 needles, cast on 100 stitches. Work 11" in garter stitch (knit every row). Tie a colored piece of yarn at the start and finish of the next row—this will show where to fold later. Work in garter stitch for another 19³/₄". Tie a colored piece of yarn at the start and finish of the next row. Work in garter stitch until the fabric measures 41³/₄" in total. Bind off.

FINISHING: To sew the cushion together, lay the knitting out flat (gently steam it with an iron at this stage). Then

above left: The simple cotton cushion seen on top of the chenille cushion emphasizes the softer, loftier texture of the chenille yarn.

above right: The back of the cotton cushion shows the simple envelope finish.

opposite: An essay in texture— the two cushions in different yarns, but knitted in the same simple garter stitch, contrasting with a loosely woven throw.

fold the work in from the first set of colored markers and stitch the two layers together at each side using yarn and a fine running stitch or backstitch. Now fold knitting in from second set of markers and stitch the seams as before, sewing through all thicknesses of the overlapping pieces to make an "envelope." Turn right side out and place pillow form inside.

FOR THE SIMPLE CHENILLE CUSHION: Use 5 x 3¹/₂oz balls Rowan *Chunky Cotton Chenille*, pair size 8 needles, sewing needle and pins, 19³/₄"-square feather pillow form

METHOD FOR THE SIMPLE CHENILLE CUSHION: Using size 8 needles, cast on 75 stitches. Work in garter stitch following the instructions for the simple cotton cushion.

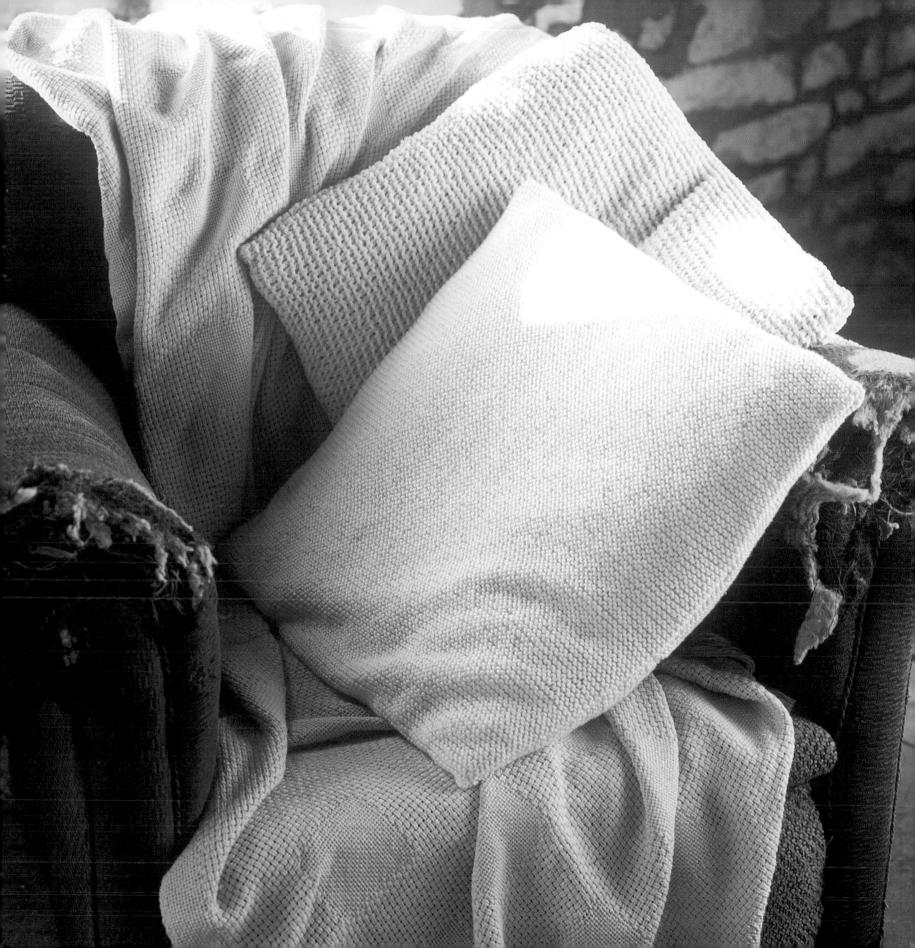

seams cushion : textured squares

This cushion is the ultimate in texture and the quickest knit ever! You just have to try knitting it.

Cozy and comfortable, the yarn is thick and softly bulky, yet so very light and airy. The cushion is

knitted on fat needles and worked in small manageable sections approximately 7½" square, which

makes it an ideal project to begin with since you can watch it grow! The finished blocks are arranged

with the "smooth" and "rough" sides of the fabric alternating in an update of popular patchwork.

The blocks are joined with outside seams to give a modern detail to this fashionable home accessory.

Several cushions in tonal shades of charcoal grays would be a cozy accompaniment nestling side by

side in a contemporary or rustic living space. For a hint of color, you could overcast the seams in a

highlight shade. Or use one of the simple alternative embroidery embellishments shown on pages

42 and 43 in a highlight color to give a seasonal accent.

how to make: **seams cushion**

FOR THE SEAMS CUSHION: Use 9 x 1³/₄oz balls Rowan *Chunky Soft*, pair size 10¹/₂ needles, sewing needle and pins, 22"-square feather pillow form

METHOD FOR THE SEAMS CUSHION: THE FRONT: Using size 10¹/₂ needles, cast on 21 stitches. Work in stockinette stitch (knit 1 row and purl the next alternately) for a total of 7¹/₂". Bind off. Work another 8 squares in stockinette stitch in exactly the same way.
THE BACK: Using size 10¹/₂ needles, cast on 61 sts. Work in garter stitch (knit every row) for a total of 2¹/₄"—this will give a firm edge. Now change to stockinette stitch (knit 1 row and purl 1 row alternately) and work until the knitting measures a total of 13". Bind off. Make another piece in exactly the same way.

above left: Simply "pinch" the two pieces together to start the seam, pin, and sew.

above center: Position the squares together with the "smooth" and the "rough" sides alternating.

above right: The back is knitted in two pieces that overlap.

opposite: Simple squares of knitting are seamed on the outside to give a textured look.

FINISHING: Lay out the 9 squares for the front in a grid 3 squares wide by 3 squares deep. You will notice that there is a "smooth" side and a "rough" side or textured side to the knitting. Reposition the "squares" so that the "smooth" side and the "rough" side of the knitting alternate. You may wish to press the squares slightly at this stage, with a steam iron, to keep flat. Thread a large needle with the yarn and sew the squares together using a fine running stitch or backstitch. Now take the 2 pieces for the back and gently steam flat. Place pieces so that the garter stitch edges overlap one another to make a back 22" square and so that one piece has the "smooth" side facing upward and the other the "rough" side; pin in position. Finally, sew the front and back together around the outer edge with all the seams on the outside. Insert the pillow form.

swatches:**embellishments**

ALTERNATIVE EMBELLISHMENTS: It is very easy to embellish your knitting. It does not have to be anything intricate, complicated or ornate; there are many ways to embroider or decorate with simple techniques. The most basic stitches inspire a variety of ideas.

Top left: Use a contrasting color of the same yarn and simply stitch diagonally in and out in running stitch across the fabric. Then go back and work a second row of stitches beside the first, keeping them irregular and "sketchy" for a rustic feel. **Top center:** For an effective hand-made or ethnic look, overcast along the join of two different colors or textures in a highlight color. **Top right:** With a contrasting or tonal color or texture use a regular running stitch to make a large cross in the middle of large squares. **Bottom left:** Outside seams look modern and functional. These could be overcast for further effect in a contrasting or tonal color. **Bottom center:** Using several strands of colored yarn, sew in and out leaving long loops on the surface. Then cut the loops, knot, and trim. **Bottom right:** Basic cross-stitch is beautifully simple on reverse textures.

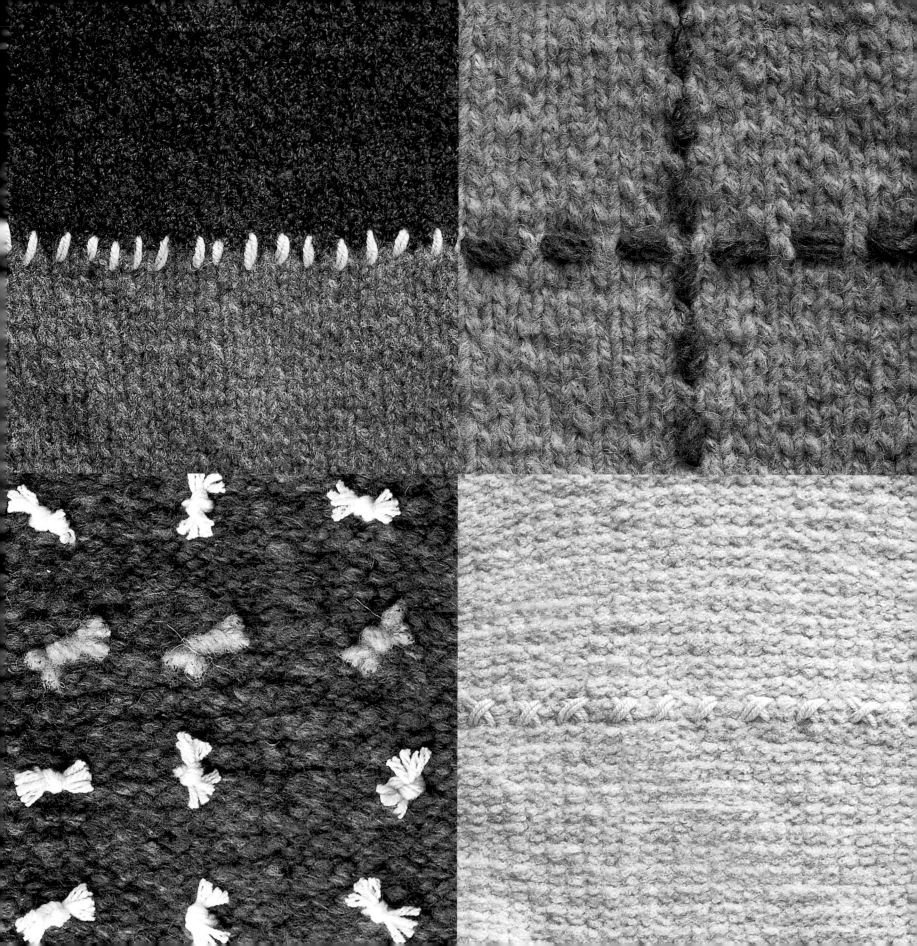

stripe cushion : string and chenille

Add stripes to your knitting! Two random strips of natural-colored string add interest to the front

of a simple contemporary cushion, especially when worked in reverse stockinette stitch. The string

gives a textural irregularity to the stripes and contrasts beautifully with the luxurious velvety pile of

the tonal-colored cotton chenille fabric. Adding stripes is a very easy technique: at the beginning of

a row just join in a new ball or length of color—the ends can be knotted or sewn into the back on

completion. Play with stripes in your knitting. If you change colors when working in stockinette stitch, the stripes will have a continuous smooth edge. But if you change shades when working in reverse stockinette stitch, the purl stitch on the right side of the fabric will produce an interesting broken line of color. The same number of rows can be used for each color or varied to give an uneven stripe repeat. The simplest line of contrasting color or texture can be amazingly effective.

how to make : **stripe cushion**

from cast-on edge. Change to light brown *Chunky Chenille* (1 strand only) and continue in stockinette stitch until the knitted piece measures a total of 44$^3/_4$" from cast-on edge. Change to 2 strands dark brown *Fine Chenille* and work 1 more row. Bind off all the stitches firmly.

FINISHING: Measure and mark two fold lines on the knitted piece—one 12$^1/_2$" from the bound-off edge (along the dark brown line) and the second 12$^1/_2$" in from the cast-on edge. With right sides of fabric facing, fold along the marked lines making sure that the dark brown bound-off edge is under the light brown cast-on edge. The two ends overlap by about 5$^1/_4$". Sew the sides of the cushion cover together through all the thicknesses, using yarn and either a fine backstitch or a fine running stitch. Turn right side out and insert the pillow form

left: A stripe of string accents the velvety chenille.

top right: Purl on the right side with a new color to create a broken line.

bottom right: The opening on the cushion back has a contrasting bound-off edge.

FOR THE STRIPE CUSHION: Use 4 x 3$^1/_2$oz balls Rowan *Chunky Cotton Chenille* in light brown and 1 x 1$^3/_4$oz ball Rowan *Fine Cotton Chenille* in dark brown, 1 small ball medium-weight string in off-white, pair size 6 needles, sewing needle and pins, 19$^3/_4$"-square feather pillow form

METHOD FOR THE STRIPE CUSHION (*worked in one piece*): Using size 6 needles and 1 strand of light brown *Chunky Chenille*, cast on 80 stitches and work 24" in stockinette stitch. Change to string and work 2 rows reverse stockinette stitch (purl right-side rows and knit wrong-side rows). Next, change back to light brown *Chunky Chenille* and work 4 rows stockinette stitch. Change to string and work 3 rows reverse stockinette stitch. Change to 2 strands dark brown *Fine Chenille* and work in stockinette stitch until knitting measures 32$^1/_4$"

swatches : stripes

ALTERNATIVE STRIPES: Introducing stripes is an easy way to give color or texture to your knitting, to use up scraps of yarn, or just to add interest. Regular or irregular; colorful, tonal, or self-colored; narrow or broad; textured or smooth—the stripe possibilities are endless.

Top left: Simply purling stitches in a new color on the right side of a stockinette stitch fabric gives an uneven, raised textural stripe. **Top center:** Knitting single rows of reverse stockinette stitch stripes at regular intervals on a piece creates a vigorous pattern. **Top right:** As a contrasting highlight on a cushion worked in rustic natural-colored string add a square of soft fur-like knitted fabric with a line of metallic thread stitched through the center. **Bottom left:** Broad, even bands of colored stripes in different stitch patterns produce an effective crisp look. **Bottom center:** Extra-wide deep tonal colors in cotton chenille make a strong contemporary impact when worked in stockinette stitch and reverse stockinette stitch. **Bottom right:** A simple raised stitch bar of seasonal color highlights large contrasting blocks of knitted color.

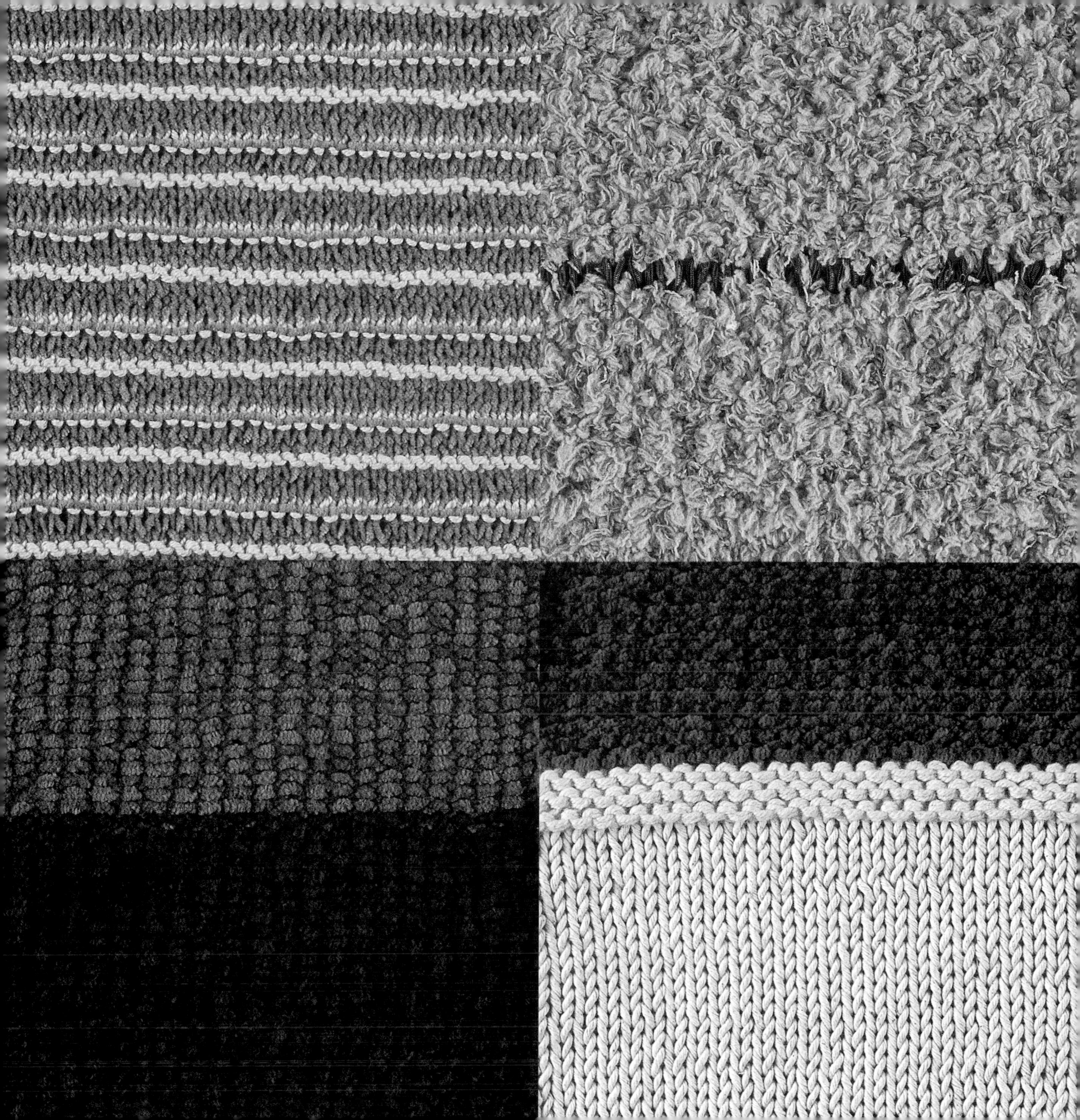

tassel throw : beaded fringe

Here is a new contemporary classic, a re-look at the traditional chenille tablecloth remembered from

the darkened parlors of ancient aunts. This one doubles as a throw for either bed or couch. It is

knitted in four long panels of alternating reverse-stockinette-stitch and stockinette-stitch squares.

The throw shown here is approximately 50½" by 44", but you can make it as small or as large as you

wish—just stop working the panel strips when you've had enough. It really couldn't be simpler. A

sumptuous material, in either cotton or viscose, chenille has its own particular characteristics. On the

plus side it has a pile like velvet, but unfortunately this pile tends to make it "spiral," and it has no

elasticity at all. So as a tip if you are having trouble obtaining a neat cast-on edge, try casting on

your stitches with a size fatter needle. Fringe the ends of the throw with lengths of chenille and

thread on, at random, simple silvered glass beads and you have a new heirloom.

how to make: tassel throw

FOR THE TASSEL THROW: Use 10 x 3¹/₂oz balls *Rowan Chunky Cotton Chenille*, pair sizes 7 and 8 needles, sewing needle and pins, crochet hook for making fringe, glass and wood beads

METHOD FOR THE TASSEL THROW: Using size 8 needles, cast on 48 stitches. Change to size 7 needles and continue as follows:
Row 1: purl 12, take yarn to back of work between two needles and knit 12, bring yarn to front of work and purl 12, take yarn to back of work and knit 12. **Rows 2–16:** repeat last row 15 more times. **Row 17:** knit 12, purl 12, knit 12, purl 12. **Rows 18–32:** repeat last row 15 more times. Now repeat the 32 rows until 16 rows of "squares" have been worked in total and knitting measures about

above left: To begin the fringe, pull doubled strands of yarn through the edge of the throw.

above center: Then slip the cut ends through the loop and pull firmly to secure.

above right: Thread beads onto the fringe and simply knot to keep in place.

opposite: The richly textured tassel throw works well thrown over couch or table.

44" from cast-on edge. Bind off using size 8 needles. Work another 3 panels in exactly the same way.

FINISHING: Sew the four panels together to form the throw, matching alternate squares. For the beaded tassels along the cast-on and bound-off ends, cut strands of yarn 12" in length. You may find it easier to wind yarn around the length of a 12" ruler and cut through both ends, to ensure that all the tassels are of a similar length. Hold 2 strands together and fold in half. Then, using a crochet hook, pull folded end through edge of work. Slip the cut ends through the folded loops and pull firmly to secure. Work a fringe sequence of doubled strands and single strands alternately. Thread beads onto single strands and knot in position randomly along the fringe.

floor cushion : stripe panels

Broad bands of fuzzy textures in subtle melanges of ivory and black via shades of flannel gray make

a contemporary textile for this luxuriously soft floor cushion. Strands of alpaca, bouclé, and chenille

are mixed together to soften the tones and create new colors. By taking one strand of two

contrasting yarns and knitting them as one you are creating unique shades and textures from

standard yarns. The blurry stripe pattern on the cushion is enormously effective yet extemely easy to

knit. Combinations of "rough" reverse stockinette stitch and "smooth" stockinette stitch textures are used for the irregular stripes. To keep track of which is the right side and which the wrong side of your knitting, be sure to mark the right side when you work your first stripe. The cushion front is made in three striped sections sewn together to form a square, and the back is worked in one piece in a single color. This is a perfect accessory in the living area for Bohemian styling in a modern setting.

how to make : floor cushion

FOR THE FLOOR CUSHION: Use 3 x 1³/₄oz balls Jaeger *Alpaca* in cream, 1 ball in light gray, and 1 ball in dark gray; 8 x 1³/₄oz balls Jaeger *Persia* in ivory, 2 balls in mid gray, and 1 ball in dark gray; 1 x 1³/₄oz ball Rowan *Fine Cotton Chenille* in black; and pair size 8 needles, sewing needle and pins, 28¹/₂"-square pillow form

COLOR KEY: Each stripe color is created by using two different strands of yarn together to make the following new texture and color combinations:

- **A (off-white)** =1 strand cream *Alpaca* and 1 strand ivory *Persia* used together
- **B (light gray)** = 1 strand light gray *Alpaca* and 1 strand mid gray *Persia* used together
- **C (charcoal)** = 1 strand dark gray *Persia* and 1 strand black *Chenille* used together (will knit slightly thicker than other colors)
- **D (pastel gray)** = 1 strand light gray *Alpaca* and 1 strand ivory *Persia* used together
- **E (dark gray)** =1 stand dark gray *Alpaca* and 1 strand dark gray *Persia used together*

left: If the row is purled on the right side of the knitted fabric when a new shade is added, a broken color line is created and a ridged texture is produced. New colors introduced in plain stockinette stitch, however, produce stripes with smooth edges and smooth surfaces.

right: Measuring about 28¹/₂" square when finished, this large luxurious cushion is knitted in soft yarn textures and tonal stripes (see page 125 for descriptions and specifications of the yarns used). The comfortable informal floor cushion is the new accessory for easy living.

METHOD FOR THE FLOOR CUSHION: THE BACK: With size 8 needles, cast on 101 stitches using A (see color key). Work in stockinette stitch for 28¹/₂". Bind off.

THE FRONT: *(worked in 3 pieces)*: The front has two side pieces and one center panel. *For each side piece*, cast on 25 stitches using size 8 needles and A. Work 18 rows A stockinette stitch, 18 rows B and 1 row A reverse stockinette stitch, 33 rows A stockinette stitch, 28 rows B and 1 row A reverse stockinette stitch, 33 rows A stockinette stitch, 18 rows B and 1 row A reverse stockinette stitch, and 17 rows A stockinette stitch. Bind off. Make second side piece the same way. *For center panel*, cast on 50 stitches using size 8 needles and D. Work 6 rows D, 6 rows C and 4 rows D stockinette stitch, 18 rows B and 1 row D reverse stockinette stitch, 3 rows D and 10 rows E stockinette stitch, (3 rows D stockinette stitch, 1 row C reverse stockinette stitch) 3 times, 8 rows D stockinette stitch, 28 rows B and 1 row D reverse stockinette stitch, 7 rows D stockinette stitch, (1 row C reverse stockinette stitch, 3 rows D stockinette stitch) 3 times, 10 rows E and 4 rows D stockinette stitch, 18 rows B and 1 row D reverse stockinette stitch, 3 rows D, 6 rows C and 6 rows D stockinette stitch. Bind off using D.

FINISHING: Sew in all yarn ends. Complete front of cushion by pinning 3 panels together with right sides facing and matching the wide B stripes. Sew the panel seams using a fine backstitch and 2 strands of cream *Alpaca*. With right sides together, pin the front piece to the back piece and sew around three sides, leaving the fourth side open. Turn right side out, insert the pillow form and sew up the last side.

table runner : stripes and beads

Once only remembered as a strip of fabric sliding over your grandmother's sideboard, anchored only

by a glass fruit bowl, the image of the table runner has changed. It is now a desirable contemporary

homeware accessory, perfect for informal dining in or out of doors. A strip of texture and color will

effectively set off and accentuate your "top of the table" crockery, tableware, glassware, and linen.

This is a simple starter project, so easy and quick to make and to coordinate to your individual table

decoration and design. Knitting this runner in your chosen shades, from classic neutral tones to strong seasonal color, is an easy way to "ring the changes" and add instant fashion to your interior. It is knitted in natural-colored string, but you could use cotton or linen yarn instead. Edged at each end with a simple border in tonal stripes, inspired by tea-towel patterns, it is further embellished with raffia and an eclectic mix of wood and glass beads for a rustic look.

how to make:**table runner**

Rows 22–26: stockinette stitch using string. **Row 27:** purl using string to make a purl bar.

Continue in stockinette stitch and string until work measures 13" from last purl bar, ending with a purl row. Using dark olive, purl across next row to make a bar, then continue in stockinette stitch until this olive section measures $9^3/4$" from the last purl bar, ending with a purl row. With string, purl across next row to make a bar, then continue in stockinette stitch until this string section measures 13" from the last purl bar, finishing with a purl row. To complete the table runner work from row 27 back to row 1 and bind off using raffia.

FINISHING: Thread beads onto lengths of fine string and attach along narrow ends of the runner. Then sew beads along third stripe from each end.

left The knitted table runner measures $14^1/2$" by 50"

top right: Match yarn to string weight by using several strands at once.

bottom right: Use fine string for threading beads.

FOR THE TABLE RUNNER: Use 1 skein ecru raffia, 6 balls medium-weight string for knitting, 3 x $1^3/4$oz balls Rowan *Cotton Glacé* in dark olive and 1 ball in light green, 1 ball fine string for attaching beads, pair size 10 needles, large sewing needle, assorted beads

METHOD FOR THE TABLE RUNNER: Using size 10 needles and raffia, cast on 45 stitches.

Rows 1–6: starting with a knit row, work 6 rows stockinette stitch using medium-weight string. **Row 7:** purl using 3 strands light green cotton yarn to make a purl bar. **Rows 8–12:** stockinette stitch using light green. **Row 13:** knit using string. **Row 14:** purl using 3 strands dark olive cotton yarn. **Row 15:** purl using dark olive to make a purl bar. **Rows 16–19:** stockinette stitch using string. **Row 20:** knit using string to make a purl bar. **Row 21:** purl using string to make a purl bar.

beaded cushions : linen or chenille

Opposites attract, so mix silk with linen, wood with metal—anything goes. Simple decorative

touches add an innovative twist to these most basic cushions. To make the "fold-over" cushion you

just knit a long "scarf" in your favorite yarn, fold it in half widthwise, seam, bead the ends, stuff

with a soft pillow form, and allow the excess fabric to flop over. The chenille reverse-stockinette-

stitch cushion is also decorated with beads, but only in the corners, and it has a simple overlapping

back opening. Your beading will be totally individual and unique—the only limitation is the strength

of your imagination. Scour secondhand shops and flea markets for old and broken bead necklaces

and vintage trimmings. Choose sumptuous textures in colors of comfort and warmth for inside, or

natural flax or bleached linen for that special evening dining al fresco. Remember, if you want to

you can make your cushion to a special size with a minimum of effort (see page 124).

how to make : **beaded cushions**

FOR THE "FOLD-OVER" CUSHION: Use 9oz of very lightweight linen yarn and small amount in a contrasting color, pair size 3 needles, sewing needle and pins, assorted beads, 15³/₄" x 11³/₄" feather pillow form

METHOD FOR THE "FOLD-OVER" CUSHION: Using size 3 needles and contrasting yarn, cast on 112 stitches. Knit 4 rows to make a garter-stitch edge. Using main yarn, work 40" stockinette stitch. Using contrasting yarn, knit 4 rows for garter-stitch edge. Bind off.

FINISHING: Gently steam work. Fold knitting in half widthwise with right sides together. Sew two side seams using fine backstitch or running stitch. Turn right side out. Insert the pillow form into the "bag," and allow excess fabric to fold over and make a flap. Sew beads all along the open end at intervals. For fringe, thread beads onto separate lengths of yarn and knot in position. Sew "strings" of beads at intervals around the garter-stitch edge.

FOR THE REVERSE-STOCKINETTE-STITCH CUSHION: Use 3 x 3¹/₂oz balls Rowan *Chunky Cotton Chenille*, pair sizes 6, 7, and 8 needles, large sewing needle and pins, beads, 15³/₄" x 11³/₄" feather pillow form

METHOD FOR THE REVERSE-STOCKINETTE-STITCH CUSHION: With size 8 needles, cast on 62 stitches. Using size 7 needles, work 26³/₄" reverse stockinette stitch, tying a colored piece of yarn to the last and first stitch when work measures 8¹/₄" and 20", to indicate where to "fold." Bind off with size 6 needle.

FINISHING: Gently steam work. Fold knitting at the fold markers so that purl sides are facing and ends overlap in the middle. Sew side seams with fine backstitch or running stitch. Turn right side out. Thread beads onto lengths of yarn, not necessarily chenille which may be too thick. Attach bead decoration to two top corners. Insert the pillow form.

opposite left: Strings of beads are attached along the edge of the "fold-over" cushion.

opposite right: Bead clusters decorate the corners of the reverse stockinette stitch cushion.

this page: The "fold-over" cushion is knitted in a fine linen yarn and the reverse-stockinette-stitch cushion in a thick cotton chenille.

swatches : beading

ALTERNATIVE BEADING: Whether your beads are wood, glass metal, stone, pearl, or ceramic, round, oval, or square, faceted or smooth, opaque, transparent, frosted, or polished, there are many ways to use them to adorn your knitting. Here are some simple bead decorations that are sewn on, not knitted in. Play with contrasting textures and colors, mixing the beads at random or organizing them in neat repeating rows.

Top left: Simple ribs in cotton ar set off here with tiny seed-like natural wood beads. **Top center:** Strands of metallic bugle beads with natural coconut drops alternate with tiny beads knotted at intervals along strings. **Top right:** For this simple fastening idea, a leather string is threaded through a button on the inside of a chenille cushion and the ends are decorated randomly with glass and wood beads. **Bottom left:** Tonal beads in simple geometric patterns and motifs create an interesting border.

Bottom center: Ordinary string threaded with raffia and rows of wood beads creates a rustic plaid. **Bottom right:** Randomly spaced between rows of purl bars, simple lines of glass beads produce a refined pattern on silk.

s l e e p i n g

squares throw : felted wool

This is it—the ultimate comfort blanket. And as an interior fashion statement it will give you an instant "home-décor magazine" look. You'll love it and it's fast to knit. Made in the lightest, loftiest and most up-to-the-minute yarn ever, this large throw is warm, cozy, and comfortable to the touch. To make it, all you do is knit blocks of stockinette-stitch and reverse-stockinette-stitch squares and sew the completed blocks together. The pattern of alternating square textures is similar to that of

the tassel throw (see pages 50–53), but the size of the squares and the feel of the yarn gives it a

completely different character. For the edging, you knit four long strips in stockinette stitch and join

them to the outer edges of the throw, butting them together at the corners. This simple border is

left to naturally roll in on itself. Although it is a project you can pick up and put down, I guarantee

that you will want to finish it and won't let it languish in a bottom drawer.

how to make: squares throw

FOR THE SQUARES THROW: Use 35 x 1^3/$_4$oz balls Rowan *Chunky Soft*, pair size 11 needles, large sewing needle and pins

METHOD FOR THE SQUARES THROW: THE CENTER SQUARES: With size 11 needles, cast on 60 stitches. **Row 1:** knit 30 stitches, then bring yarn to front of work between two needles and purl 30 stitches. Repeat previous row, so that 30 stitches are worked in stockinette stitch and 30 stitches are worked in reverse stockinette stitch, until work measures 12" from cast-on edge. **Next row:** to make the check effect you must now purl the first 30 stitches and knit the next 30 stitches. Repeat the previous row until work measures 24" in total from cast-on edge. Bind off. Make a total of 9 of these squares.

above left: The trim is made of long strips of stockinette stitch, butted together at the corners, and is left to roll in on itself.

above right: The pattern of squares of stockinette stitch and reverse stockinette stitch.

opposite: Soft, textured yarn set off by crisp fresh linen creates a very modern look—plain and simple comfort. The finished squares throw measures approximately 72" by 72".

TRIM: With size 11 needles, cast on 5 stitches. Work in stockinette stitch, slipping the first stitch and knitting the last stitch of each row to give neat, firm edges. Work 4 strips in this way, each 70^3/$_4$" long.

FINISHING: Sew in all ends by weaving along knitting not along edge. Lay each "square" out flat and gently steam. Then lay out the 9 squares in a grid 3 squares wide by 3 squares deep. Pin the squares together, making sure that stitches alternate to make a pattern. Sew squares together by overcasting the seams on the inside. Pin a trim-strip to one side of throw so that strip extends 1^1/$_2$" past one end. Pin second strip in place all along next side, sewing one end to overlap and letting strip extend 1^1/$_2$" past other end. Sew on third and fourth strips in the same way.

felted sweater : an old friend

This is what I call an "old friend" sweater. The kind that is always there for you—cozy to scramble

hurriedly into on chilly weekend mornings, to relax into when free from work, or to travel in as your

comforter—a timeless classic. Made oversize to fit all, it is worked in five easy rectangles of

stockinette stitch—a back and front, two sleeves, and a collar. Worked in a thick, soft felted yarn,

the rectangles grow fast on the needles. Side slits and a cowl neck are all that it needed to give a

sense of style to the very simplistic shape, and the outside seam details add a unique character. My

one finishing tip is to use a wool yarn in a matching color for joining seams, since the loftiness of the

felted yarn can make it fray or separate when it is used for stitching. If you choose to make the felted

sweater in a soft neutral gray it will become a seasonal piece, in black a classic. But whatever shade

you choose, I'm sure you'll still be wearing it ten years from now!

how to make: felted sweater

FOR THE FELTED SWEATER: Use 17 x 1³/₄oz balls Rowan *Chunky Soft*, pair size 11 needles, large sewing needle and pins

METHOD FOR THE FELTED SWEATER: BACK: With size 11 needles, cast on 62 stitches. Begin the ribbing with a right-side row as follows:
Rib row 1: (purl 2, knit 1) to last 2 stitches, purl 2. **Rib row 2:** (knit 2, purl 1) to last 2 stitches, knit 2.
Now work ribbed side slits integrally by keeping first 5 stitches and last 5 stitches on needle in rib (as set in first 2 rows) and stitches in between in stockinette stitch until back measures 7" from cast-on edge. Then work all 62 stitches in stockinette stitch until back measures 16¹/₂" from cast-on edge. Place colored strand of yarn at each end of last row for position of armholes. Continue in stockinette stitch until back measures 27". Bind off.
THE FRONT: Work the front exactly as for the back.
THE SLEEVES *(2 the same):* Using size 11 needles, cast on 53 stitches. Work 2 rows of ribbing as for back. Then beginning with a knit row, work in stockinette stitch until sleeve measures 18" from cast-on edge. Bind off.
THE COLLAR: With size 11 needles, cast on 61 stitches. Work in stockinette stitch for 8¹/₄". Bind off.

FINISHING: Lay each piece out and gently steam flat. With wrong sides facing, pin front and back together at shoulders. Leaving neck opening in the middle, stitch 6" at each side using yarn and a very fine running stitch—these seams will be on the outside of the sweater. Sew each sleeve in place in between markers using very fine running stitch and again with seam on outside of the sweater. Fold sweater in half at shoulder so that right sides are together and sew sleeve seams and side seams above "slit" trim. Turn the sweater right side out. For the collar, pin and stitch the center back collar seam so that the collar forms a ring. Then pin smooth side of collar to the inside of the neck edge, and sew collar into opening using running stitch and leaving seam to show on the outside as detail. Fold collar toward the outside, and turn back cuffs.

opposite left: A few stitches in rib along the side slits are just one of the details that give the sweater a sense of style.

opposite right: Sew the seams so that they show on the outside and are invisible on the inside as instructed.

this page: This functional yet fashionably "felted" oversize sweater measures 45½" in circumference and is 27" long.

color-block throw : tonal grays

Simply graphic, modern and minimal, clean and chic, this throw is an absolutely essential home accessory. Its refined elegance will add a touch of contemporary classicism to any of the comfort zones in your house. Knitted in four separate blocks of monochromatic color that are stitched together when complete, the throw uses a soft extra-fine merino wool for three of the large squares and a contrasting bouclé texture for the fourth. Merino wool is a high quality yarn that is beautiful

to touch, so a joy to work with. And because it has a smooth surface and a subtle sheen, it gives great stitch definition—just the thing to add elegance to a simple design. A garter-stitch border is integrated into each square, so there's no trim to add around the edge later. Here's your opportunity to try out alternative yarns on an easy pattern. To really pamper yourself, what about knitting the throw in the noble yarns—alpaca, cashmere, or angora.

how to make : color-block throw

FOR THE COLOR-BLOCK THROW: Use 8 x 1³/₄oz balls of Jaeger *Extra Fine Merino* each in off-white, light gray, and charcoal, and 5 x 1³/₄oz balls Jaeger *Persia* in mid gray, pair sizes 6 and 7 needles, large sewing needle and pins

METHOD FOR COLOR-BLOCK THROW: THE MERINO SQUARES: Using size 6 needles and off-white *Merino*, cast on 176 stitches and work 2¹/₂" garter stitch (knit every row). Then begin with a right-side row as follows:
Next row (right side): knit to end of row. **Next row:** knit 13, purl to last 13 stitches, knit 13.
Keep repeating last 2 rows (so that 13 stitches at beginning and end of row are garter stitch and center 150 stitches are stockinette stitch) until work measures 29" from cast-on edge. Now work 2¹/₂" garter stitch. Bind off.

above left: Three knitted blocks in extra-fine merino wool are highlighted by the fourth block in a fuzzy bouclé. The joined blocks form a throw that measures 63" square.

above right: The integral edge of garter stitch provides a precision border to each square.

opposite: Relaxed and easy elegance, a simple throw to cover bed, chair, or couch in the contemporary home.

Work 2 more squares in exactly the same way, but using light gray for one and charcoal for the other.
THE PERSIA SQUARE: Using size 7 needles and mid gray *Persia*, cast on 128 stitches and work 2¹/₂" garter stitch. Then begin with a right-side row as follows:
Next row (right side): knit to end of row. **Next row:** knit 9, purl to last 9 stitches, knit 9.
Keep repeating last 2 rows (so that 9 stitches at beginning and end of row are garter stitch and center 110 stitches are stockinette stitch) until work measures 29" from cast-on edge. Now work 2¹/₂" garter stitch. Bind off.

FINISHING: Lay pieces flat and gently steam into shape. Pin the 4 squares together, making sure that all the edges match. Sew all seams using a fine running stitch.

button cushions : stitch textures

Choose from a variety of stitch patterns for this tailored cushion—smooth stockinette stitch, or a

textured seed stitch, rib stitch, or check stitch. And there's nothing stopping you from trying other

simple stitch patterns, like garter stitch, other rib stitch variations or even reverse stockinette stitch.

But be sure to use a good quality yarn—the better the yarn, the better the finish. The pattern calls

for a merino wool, but alpaca or cashmere are also perfect for this project. For a more casual or rustic

environment, you could try a tweedy linen or string. A group of cushions in different stitches but the

same yarn and color would look good on a bed, or in different yarn textures on a couch. Sew on

beautifully simple natural mother of pearl buttons in ivory or charcoal to add the perfect finish. Or,

hunt for wonderful individual buttons in secondhand shops or flea markets. This is the final detail

that really counts. Take a look at pages 86 and 87 for more button and yarn combination ideas.

how to make : button cushions

FOR THE BUTTON CUSHIONS: Use 6 x 1³/₄oz balls of Jaeger *Extra Fine Merino* for each cushion, pair sizes 5 and 6 needles, sewing needle and pins, 5 x ³/₄" buttons, 15³/₄"-square feather pillow form

STITCH CHOICES FOR THE BUTTON CUSHIONS:
STOCKINETTE STITCH PATTERN: Knit 1 row and purl 1 row alternately.
SEED STITCH PATTERN: Row 1: *purl 1, knit 1, repeat from * to end. **Row 2:** knit the purl stitches and purl the knit stitches as they appear. Repeat row 2 to form the pattern.
RIB PATTERN: Row 1: knit 2, (purl 2, knit 3) to last 3 stitches, purl 2, knit 1. **Row 2:** purl 1, (knit 2, purl 3) to last 4 stitches, knit 2, purl 2. Repeat last 2 rows to form the pattern.
CHECK PATTERN: Row 1: (knit 5, purl 5) to end. **Rows 2, 3, and 4:** as row 1. **Row 5:** (purl 5, knit 5) to end. **Rows 6, 7, and 8:** as row 5. Repeat these 8 rows to form the pattern.

METHOD FOR THE BUTTON CUSHIONS: THE BACK: With size 6 needles, cast on 90 stitches and work 15³/₄" in your chosen stitch pattern (see above), finishing with a wrong-side row. With the right side facing and starting with a knit row, begin the button band by working 10 rows stockinette stitch, ending with a purl row. With the right side (or the "smooth" side) of the knitting facing you and using size 5 needles, work a purl row across the stitches for a very neat "folding" row. Change back to size 6 needles, and starting with a purl row, work in stockinette stitch for 10 more rows. Bind off.
THE FRONT: Work the first 15³/₄" as for the back, finishing with a wrong-side row. Then with the right side facing and starting with a knit row, begin the buttonhole band by working 4 rows stockinette stitch, finishing with a purl row. Next, work the buttonholes as follows:
Buttonhole row 1 (right side): knit first 8 stitches, bind off next 3 stitches, (knit until there are 15 stitches on right-hand needle after last bind-off, bind off the next 3 stitches) 4 times, knit last 7 stitches. **Butthonhole row 2:** Purl across row, casting on 3 stitches over those bound-off in previous row.
Work 4 more rows stockinette stitch, finishing with a purl row. Using size 5 needles, work a purl row across the stitches. Change back to size 6 needles and starting with a purl row, work 4 rows stockinette stitch, then work another set of buttonholes as before in line over the previous set. Work 4 rows stockinette stitch. Bind off.

FINISHING: Gently steam into shape. Pin back and front with right sides together, and use a fine running stitch to join three sides, leaving the buttonhole side open. Next, fold the button bands in half along the purl-stitch row, and sew to the inside. Turn cushion right side out and sew on the buttons to correspond with the buttonholes.

top left: Knit a double row of buttonholes. When the cushion pieces are joined, fold the bands to the inside.

bottom left: The ribbed button cushion and a stockinette-stitch chenille alternative with a single stripe.

center left: Stitch the buttonholes together with buttonhole stitch and sew the buttons to the inside of the band.

opposite: Mixing alternative versions of the cushion adds style. Try it in other yarns for contrasting textures.

swatches:buttons

ALTERNATIVE BUTTONS: Think of buttons as not only functional fastening devices, but as prime decoration as well. They add character and stylish detail and can make or break your knitted garment or accessory. Take the time to look at the enormous variety of buttons that are available to you—horn, bone, wood, shell, nut, glass, ceramic, or synthetic. As a simple tip, remember that buttons with sewing holes will sit more snuggly on stretchy knitwear than those with protruding shanks.

Top left: Natural horn buttons on textured bouclé. **Top center:** Metal or metal-look buttons on tweed create a vibrant contrast. **Top right:** Coconut shell buttons have been used in many cultures, but now come mostly from Asia. They are shown here on knitted string. Use the reverse side to give a two-tone effect. **Bottom left:** Mother-of-pearl here picks up all the lights in a color on silk. **Bottom center:** Troche pearl buttons from Asia on merino wool. Cream or smoky gray shades go with all colors. **Bottom right:** Mollusk shell buttons work exceptionally well on textured linen.

child's blanket : ridged stripes

Here's a new hand-me-down for for the stroller or crib, perfect for a child to cuddle up in, snug and

contented, for an afternoon nap. The blanket is knitted in a solid color with thin garter-stitch ridged

stripes at the ends and a symphony of tonal blue and ecru textured stripes in the center. For the very

simple colored stripes, all you do is join in a new color with each row, choosing the yarns at random.

The ridged texture comes from mixing one or two rows of "rough" reverse stockinette stitch into

the "smooth" stockinette stitch. Although the random stripes have an overall consistency, there's no symmetry—so you can't go wrong with your knitting! Garter-stitch trim sewn to the finished blanket adds stylish detail and secures the otherwise loose edges. Making this project can be a good way to use up yarn left over from other knits. Why not try it in other color schemes, substituting the smooth cotton used here for different, more fuzzy fiber textures.

how to make: child's blanket

FOR THE CHILD'S BLANKET: Use 10 x 1³/₄oz balls Rowan *Handknit D.K. Cotton* in ecru and 1 ball each in navy, ice blue, and beige, and 1 x 3¹/₂oz ball Rowan *Chunky Cotton Chenille* in lavender, pair sizes 3 and 5 needles, sewing needle and pins

METHOD FOR THE CHILD'S BLANKET: THE CENTER OF BLANKET: Using size 5 needles and ecru *Handknit D.K. Cotton*, cast on 130 stitches. Still using the ecru cotton, work the first 48 rows of border as follows:
Starting with a knit (right-side) row, work 6 rows in stockinette stitch (knit 1 row and purl 1 row alternately), mark the right side with a colored thread, then work 2 rows in garter stitch (knit every row), 2 rows in stockinette stitch, 2 rows in garter stitch, 6 rows in stockinette stitch, 4 rows in garter stitch, 8 rows in stockinette stitch, 2 rows in garter stitch, 4 rows in stockinette stitch, 4 rows in garter stitch, and 8 rows in stockinette stitch.

Next, begin the textured stripe section of the blanket using 5 different yarns for the stripes—ecru, navy, ice blue, and beige *Handknit D.K. Cotton*, and lavender *Chunky Cotton Chenille*. Work the stripes in a random pattern, changing the yarn on every row and randomly working a few rows in stockinette stitch alternating with 1 or 2 rows in reverse stockinette stitch (purl right-side rows and knit wrong-side rows). Work a total of 148 rows in stripes in this way.
Now knit the 48 rows of the final border in ecru *Handknit D.K. Cotton* as follows:
Starting with a knit (right-side) row, work 8 rows in stockinette stitch, 4 rows in garter stitch, 4 rows in stockinette stitch, 2 rows in garter stitch, 2 rows in stockinette stitch, 2 rows in garter stitch, 8 rows in stockinette stitch, 2 rows in garter stitch, 4 rows in stockinette stitch, 4 rows in garter stitch, and 8 rows in stockinette stitch. Bind off.

FINISHING: Sew in all loose ends of yarn. Lay work out flat and steam gently. Next, work the trim for the blanket as follows:
THE TRIM: Using size 3 needles and ecru *Handknit D.K. Cotton*, cast on 9 stitches. Knit every row for about 32¹/₂"—this strip should fit neatly along one long side edge of the blanket. Bind off. Make another strip the same length. Evenly pin one of these trim strips to each long side edge of the blanket and overcast in place. Then make another 2 strips in the same way, each about 28¹/₄" long—each of these strips should fit neatly along one short side of the blanket including the ends of the trim strips. Pin these strips to the top and bottom edges of the blanket and overcast. Sew the ends of the strips together where they meet.

top left: The top and bottom ends of the blanket have textured borders worked in a single color. Purl rows create surface relief.

bottom left: Neaten the edges of the finished blanket by adding the garter stitch trim. Butt the trim ends together at the four corners.

center left: When working the simple stripes at the center of the blanket, join in yarns at will; the random use of color adds energy to the design.

opposite: The solid-colored borders and trim soften the energetic stripes. The finished child's blanket measures approximately 28¹/₄" by 35¹/₂".

child's cushion : embroidery

Childlike outlines of flowers, cats, little houses, and stars come to life on these denim-yarn cushions.

Use your children's or your niece's, nephew's, or grandchild's drawings to inspire your simple, innocent motifs. Or, record your own childhood memories in this fun and practical way. The denim yarn used is hardwearing and playful and fades in the rough and tumble of everyday living. It is great for children's projects and rooms. Accent an indigo denim-yarn cushion with ecru embroidery

motifs or an ecru denim-yarn cushion with the indigo. Keep the motifs simple and fresh and they'll

be easy to embroider in backstitch. An even easier way to embroider line drawings on knitting is to

outline the shapes in fine running stitch, then go back over the shapes with a second row of running

stitch filling in the spaces left on the first journey. Maybe your child would like to have a go at the

embroidery! It's a good introduction to the fun of stitching.

how to make: child's cushion

FOR THE CHILD'S CUSHION: Use 9 x 1³/₄oz balls Rowan *Denim* in main color (indigo or ecru) and 1 ball in contrasting color (ecru or indigo), pair size 6 needles, large blunt-ended sewing needle and pins, 19³/₄"-square feather pillow form

METHOD FOR THE CHILD'S CUSHION: Using size 6 needles, cast on 100 stitches and work in stockinette stitch until knitting measures 23¹/₂" from cast-on edge (this allows for shrinkage—*see below*). Bind off. Make another piece in exactly the same way.

FINISHING: The *Denim* yarn shrinks in length the first time it is washed, so before sewing the cushion pieces together they must be washed. First, loosely

above left: Embroidering your knitting is a very simple way of enhancing a design.

above center: You may need to use two or three strands of yarn to make the motifs stand out.

above right: Frame the cushion front with an outline of bold blanket stitches.

opposite: Fill in backgrounds with widely spaced stars made up of simple straight stitches.

wind some of the contrasting yarn into a small ball or hank. Then wash and dry the knitted pieces and the small ball at the same time, carefully following the instructions on the yarn label. Lay the pieces flat and gently steam, pulling them into shape. Using a large blunt-ended needle and contrasting yarn doubled, embroider one piece with simple motifs in fine backstitch; the cushions shown provide some inspiration. If you like, work motif details with other simple embroidery stitches. After the embroidery is complete, pin the two cushion pieces right sides together and join three sides with a fine running stitch. Turn right side out, insert pillow form and sew up the opening. Work blanket stitch all around the cushion using a single strand of contrasting yarn.

simple slippers : seed stitch

These are the sweetest soft baby slippers you'll ever see! They are so irresistible that even having to

work the simple increasing and decreasing techniques won't put you off. Make them as a baby gift

or knit an adult size for yourself or your partner. Handmade gifts are the best, and these relaxed

indoor shoes with their pared-down design are sure to be treasured. The baby sizes can be knitted

in either a denim yarn or a simple cotton knitting yarn, and the two adult sizes in denim yarn.

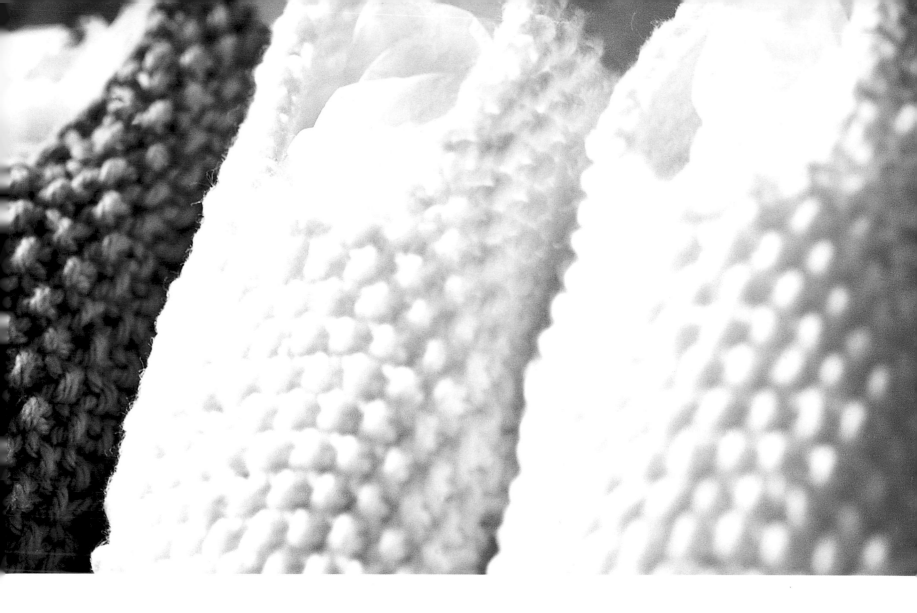

Although the denim yarn shrinks in length when it is first washed, this is no problem since the shrinkage is compensated for in the knitting pattern. Denim has an especially seductive feel and look, and gives the slippers extra firmness, so its worth that little extra care needed for washing and drying the pieces before stitching them together. Worked completely in beautiful textural seed stitch, these slippers are ideal for the bathroom or bedroom, or for lounging around the house.

how to make : simple slippers

FOR THE BABY SLIPPERS: Use 1 x 1³/₄oz ball Rowan *Handknit D.K. Cotton* or 1 x 1³/₄oz ball Rowan *Denim*, pair size 5 needles, sewing needle and pins

FOR THE ADULT SLIPPERS: Use 2 x 1³/₄oz balls Rowan *Denim* in ecru, pair size 5 needles, large sewing needle and pins

SEED STITCH PATTERN: *(over odd number of stitches)* **Row 1:** knit 1, *purl 1, knit 1, repeat from * to end. **Row 2:** knit the purl stitches and purl the knit stitches as they appear. Repeat row 2 to form the pattern.

METHOD FOR THE SLIPPERS: The pattern is written for the baby's size and the instructions for the adult's small and adult's medium follow inside brackets []; where there is only one figure, it applies to all sizes.

THE SOLES *(2 the same)*: Using size 5 needles, cast on 9 [11: 11] stitches and work 1 row seed stitch. **Baby version only:** Working the whole sole in seed stitch, increase 1 stitch at each end

of next row by knitting into front and back of first and last stitch. (11 stitches on needle.) Work 3¹/₂" without shaping for *D.K. Cotton* and 4" for *Denim*. Decrease 1 stitch at each end of row by knitting first 2 stitches together and last 2. **Adult versions only:** Working the whole sole in seed stitch, cast on 2 stitches at each end of next row. (15 [15] stitches on needle.) Work 8¹/₂" [9¹/₂"] without shaping. Bind off 2 stitches at start of each of next 2 rows. **Both versions:** Bind off remaining 9 [11: 11] stitches in seed stitch.

THE UPPERS *(2 the same)*: Using size 5 needles, cast on 19 [41: 41] stitches. Working the whole upper in seed stitch, increase 1 stitch at end of next row by knitting into front and back of last stitch, then increase 1 stitch at same edge on the next 5 rows for the toe shaping. (25 [47: 47] stitches on needle.) Work 4 [10: 10] rows without shaping, finishing at straight back edge. Bind off 12 [23: 23] stitches in seed stitch at start of next row. Decrease 1 stitch at end of next row by knitting last 2 stitches together. Decrease 1 stitch at start of next row by knitting first 2 stitches together. Increase 1 stitch at end of next row by casting on 1 stitch after last stitch. Work 1 row without shaping. Cast on 13 [24: 24] stitches at end of next row. (25 [47: 47] stitches on needle.) Work 4 [10: 10] rows without shaping. Decrease 1 stitch at toe end on next 6 rows. Bind off remaining 19 [41: 41] stitches.

FINISHING: For denim yarn, wash and dry all parts of the slippers according to yarn label before sewing up to allow for shrinkage. Join straight edges at back of heel on uppers. Insert sole, pin around edge, and attach using simple blanket stitch, easing in fullness around toe.

top left: Increase one stitch by working into the front and back of the same stitch (top), or several by casting on stitches (bottom).

bottom left: The finished adult slippers are 3³/₄" wide, and either 7" or 8" long. Because they are worked in seed stitch they are very stretchy.

center left: The slipper sole (left) and upper (right). Join straight ends of the upper before stitching on the sole.

opposite: Baby slippers in shades of blue and ecru cotton yarn. Knit them in denim yarn or simple cotton yarn.

bathing

wash mitt : rustic sisal string

String provides the simplest and most basic yarn to knit in tonal colors from white, ecru, and straw

to soft mellow golds. Rich in variety of texture, from fine cabled parcel strings, soft furry garden

twines to coarsely textured rustic sisal—string has endless possibilities for the interior. Its simplicity

adds an honesty to many homeware products all around the house from the living areas to the

bathroom, and from cushions and table runners to this authentic wash mitt. The wash mitt is worked

in sisal string in simple rows of knit and purl. It is a little hard on the hands to work with at first but has a great effect on the body. Being naturally abrasive, it sloughs and softens. The wash mitt is very easy to make, as it is knitted in one piece, folded over, then sewn together. This mitt measures 8" by 6", but you could create a continuous long piece to use as a back scrubber. Either, with a piece of handmade soap, would make a great gift for a friend.

how to make : **wash mitt**

seams. Fold the knitting in half widthwise, with the rougher side of work on the outside. Pin together before stitching if you wish. Use a running stitch to sew the side seams, leaving the end opposite the fold open. Now turn the mitt right side out. You may find it easier to push the "corners" of the mitt to the inside first with the top of the knitting needle. If you like, make a loop for hanging the mitt by casting on 18 stitches (for a 10"-long cord) and binding them off in the first row. Sew both ends of the completed cord to the end of one seam.

ALTERNATIVE METHOD FOR THE WASH MITT: As an alternative you can work the mitt in two pieces $8^1/4$" by $6^3/4$" each and sew them together with the rougher side on the outside, working the seams on the outside as a detail.

left: String is the most basic of "yarns." A rich source of natural texture and color, it is inexpensive and durable.

top right: Use a single strand (of the string) to sew up the seams.

far right: Rustic sisal is a natural abrasive to slough and soften the skin.

FOR THE WASH MITT: Use two balls of rustic sisal string available from most hardware stores (the coarser the better), the largest needles you can find, probably size 15, large sewing needle

METHOD FOR THE WASH MITT: Cast on 12 stitches. Have a little patience, as the string will naturally twist and turn. Knit the first row and purl the next row. Just keep doing this—knitting 1 row and purling the next alternately—until your knitting measures $15^1/2$". Bind off the stitches on the needle. You may find the sisal a little hard to work with and control. Try wrapping the string loosely around the needle; it will then be much easier to pull through.

FINISHING: Cut a length of string from the ball. Then unravel one strand of the string to use for sewing the

"bain" bag : cool cotton

This small, decorative project is knitted in a cotton yarn that is between a sport and worsted weight

in thickness. It is worked in an attractive textured seed stitch and has a stockinette-stitch hem at the

top which is doubled over to provide a channel for a knitted or twisted drawstring. Because of its

depth and sculptural quality, the single-row blue seed-stitch stripe has the tactile look of embroidery.

A separate panel for the simple cross-stitch word is worked in stockinette stitch and joined to the

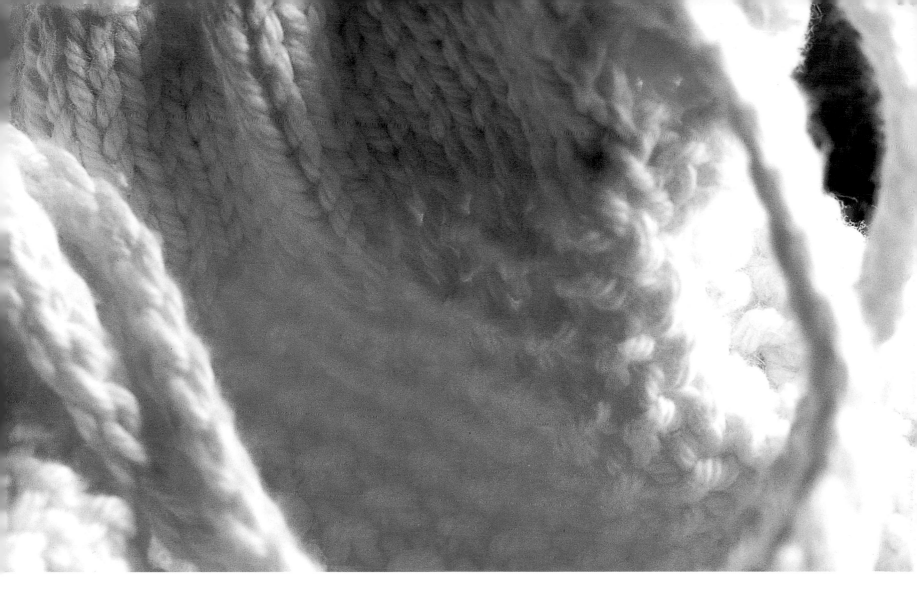

front. The distinctive word "bain" has been chosen here for the embroidery, but you could stitch alternative words such as "soap" or "l'eau," or you may even wish to personalize the bag further with family initials or children's names, to hang in a row in the bathroom. Use this simple bag as inspiration for a larger bag for underwear or socks, or work a bag in a finer stockinette stitch and embroider directly onto it. Have fun customizing!

how to make: "bain" bag

WORD PANEL: Using size 5 needles and ecru, cast on 30 stitches, work 2³/₄" stockinette stitch. Bind off. Using ice blue yarn doubled, embroider the word "bain" in cross-stitch or use your own design.

DRAWSTRING: Make a simple twisted cord 36" long. Or, make cord shown by casting on 170 stitches and binding them off in the first row, then knitting into each cast-on stitch along the other side and binding off as they are picked up.

FINISHING: Press pieces. Stitch the word panel to the front, using a fine running stitch. With right sides facing, stitch back and front pieces together along the seed stitch only, using a fine backstitch. Turn right side out. Turn hem to the inside along the foldline and sew to the inside. Thread the drawstring through top of bag and knot ends.

top left: Leave the ends of the stockinette stitch drawstring casing open when sewing the back and front together.

bottom left: Thread the drawstring through the top hem, pull the ends and tie them in a simple knot or bow.

right: The finished seed-stitch bag measures 10¹/₂" by 11¹/₂".

FOR THE "BAIN" BAG: Use 3 x 1³/₄oz balls Rowan *Handknit D.K. Cotton* in ecru and 1 ball in ice blue, pair size 5 needles, sewing needle and pins

METHOD FOR THE "BAIN" BAG: THE FRONT AND BACK (*2 pieces the same*): Using size 5 needles and ecru, cast on 50 stitches. Work seed stitch as follows:
Row 1: *knit 1, purl 1, repeat from * to end. **Row 2:** purl the knit stitches and knit the purl stitches as they appear. Repeat row 2 until knitting measures 2". Change to ice blue and work 1 row in seed stitch. Change back to ecru and continue in seed stitch until knitting measures 10¹/₂" from cast-on edge. Work 1" stockinette stitch, ending with a purl row. With right side (smooth side) of work facing, work a purl row to create a neat folding line for hem. Starting with a purl row, continue in stockinette stitch for 1" more. Bind off.

cuddle coat : soft chenille

The name says it all—a velvet-soft jacket to wrap around you when emerging from the bath or to

snuggle and cuddle in while just relaxing at home. It is knitted in a bulky cotton chenille, which is

naturally soft and absorbent and has a feel of luxury. Three-quarter sleeves and patch pockets add

fashionable detail to this loose and comfortable knit. You may even decide it is too cozy to stay in

the bathroom and make one in a classic elephant gray for chilly evenings out! So easy and quick to

knit in basic squares and no shaping! A characteristic of chenille is that it looks a little uneven in knitting, which I think is part of its charm. To add a beautiful refined quality to the finished piece, a simple tip has been followed—avoid ribbing. Traditional ribbed edges can look untidy in chenille, so here the edges have been kept deliberately plain with little side slits and simple facings. The result is extremely neat, especially when offset with large natural troche pearl buttons.

how to make : cuddle coat

FOR THE CUDDLE COAT: Use 10 x 3½oz balls Rowan *Chunky Cotton Chenille*, pair sizes 6 and 8 needles, 2 large buttons, large sewing needle and pins

METHOD FOR THE CUDDLE COAT: THE BACK: With size 8 needles, cast on 96 stitches. Change to size 6 needles and work in stockinette stitch until back measures 18" from cast-on edge. Place colored thread of yarn at each end of last row for position of armholes. Continue in stockinette stitch until back measures a total of 28". Bind off with size 8 needle. Mark 24 center stitches at bound-off edge with colored threads for neck opening.

THE RIGHT FRONT: With size 8 needles, cast on 61 stitches. Change to size 6 needles. **Row 1 (right side):** knit 8, purl 1, knit to end. **Row 2:** purl to last 9 stitches, knit 1, purl 8. Repeat last 2 rows until front measures 8" from cast-on edge, ending with a purl row. **Buttonhole row 1 (right side):** knit 2, bind off next 4 stitches (3 stitches now on right-hand needle), knit 1, purl 1, knit 2, bind off next 4 stitches, knit to end. **Buttonhole row 2:** purl to first 4 bound-off stitches, cast on 4 stitches, purl 2, knit 1, purl 2, cast on 4 stitches over bound-off stitches, purl 2. Continuing in stockinette stitch (with the single purl stitch stitch for facing foldline) for the whole front, work until front measures 16" from cast-on edge, ending with a purl row. Make another pair of buttonholes as before. Then work until front measures 18" from cast-on edge, and place colored thread of yarn at armhole edge of last row for position of armhole. Continue until front measures 25½" from cast-on edge, ending with a purl row. **Neck shaping row (right side):** bind off first 25 stitches for neck shaping, knit to end. Continue on remaining 36 stitches in stockinette stitch only until front measures same as back to shoulder. Bind off with size 8 needle.

THE LEFT FRONT: Work as for right front, but omit buttonholes, work purl foldline on opposite side, and bind off for neck shaping on a purl row.

THE SLEEVES (*2 the same*): With size 8 needles, cast on 80 stitches. Change to size 6 needles and work in stockinette stitch until sleeve measures 12". Bind off with size 8 needle.

THE POCKETS (*2 the same*): With size 8 needles, cast on 28 stitches. Change to size 6 needles and work in stockinette stitch for 6½", ending with a knit row. Knit next row for foldline, then continue in stockinette stitch until work measures 9" in total. Bind off with size 8 needle.

THE COLLAR: Using size 8 needles, cast on 80 stitches. Change to size 6 needles and work in stockinette stitch for 3", ending with a knit row. Knit next row for foldline, then begin with a knit row and continue for another 3" in stockinette stitch. Bind off with size 8 needle.

FINISHING: Sew in all ends on wrong side of knitting. Gently steam all pieces into shape. With right sides together and using backstitch, join shoulder seams, set in sleeves between colored markers, then join side and sleeve seams leaving 2¾" open at each lower edge for side slits. Fold front facing-bands to the inside along purl foldline and stitch to inside. Matching the center of collar to center back neck, ease and sew collar in place. Fold collar to inside along purl foldline and stitch. Fold pocket flaps to inside along foldline and sew to fronts of coat. Finally, sew on the two buttons to correspond to the buttonholes and cuddle up!

opposite top: Two sets of buttonholes are worked on each side of a simple purl stitch, which creates a neat foldline for the facing.

opposite below: For neatness, overcast around the double buttonholes or use a blanket stitch.

this page: Soft velvet-touch cotton chenille is quick to knit and perfect to snuggle into after bathing or on waking in the early morning. (See page 125 for finished measurements.)

knitted baskets : seed stitch

Baskets are so easy to make—simply knit five squares! Worked in seed stitch for strength and

texture, and string for practicality and color, these baskets are both useful and decorative. You can

sew the pieces together with the seams on the outside for a square box or turn inside out for a

rounded dish or basket shape. Experiment with different sizes, tiny and tall, or even try a lid to top

it off! Try indigo yarn and add starch to the final wash for extra rigidity. Use leather thonging or

raffia to create quite a different effect for another area of the house. These baskets will be functional in the bathroom, modern in the living area, and fun in the playroom. There is no end to the designs you could attempt, for example you could add single rows of color to stripe and edge the baskets or decorate with simple embroidery. This is a great first knitting project for children to make for their treasures and trinkets.

how to make:knitted baskets

FOR THE SMALL BASKET: Use 3 balls medium-weight string, pair size 6 needles, large sewing needle and pins

METHOD FOR THE SMALL BASKET: With size 6 needles, cast on 19 stitches and work in seed stitch as follows: **Row 1:** knit 1, *purl l, knit 1, repeat from * to end. Repeat the last row until 30 rows have been worked from the cast-on edge and a square has been formed. Bind off in seed stitch. Make 4 more square pieces the same.

FINISHING: Sew in all ends. Wash pieces in warm water (104°F). If extra firmness is required, add starch to the water after rinsing. Pull pieces into shape and allow to dry flat; do NOT dry in a dryer. Using string, sew each of the 4 sides together with backstitch to make an open box.

top left: Pinch the seams together and backstitch in place, or use running stitch, then go back over the stitches filling in the empty spaces (called double running stitch).

top right: Experiment with different sizes, yarns, textures, colors, and even shapes.

opposite: The finished small knitted basket measures 4³/₄" by 4³/₄" by 4³/₄", and the large basket measures 7" by 7" by 7".

Sew this joined piece to the base, leaving seams on the outside. Spray finished box with more starch if required.

FOR THE LARGE BASKET: Use 5 balls medium-weight string, pair size 6 needles, large sewing needle and pins

METHOD FOR THE LARGE BASKET: With size 6 needles, cast on 25 stitches and work in seed stitch as follows: **Row 1:** knit 1, *purl l, knit 1, repeat from * to end. Repeat the last row until 40 rows have been worked from the cast-on edge and a square has been formed. Bind off in seed stitch. Make 4 more square pieces the same.

FINISHING: Sew in all ends. Wash, shape, and sew the 5 pieces together exactly as for the small box.

rag rug : mixed textures

Cotton, terry cloth, muslin, seersucker, string, ribbon, chenille—collect all your materials together

with color and texture in mind for this rag rug. Use scraps of fabric and leftover yarn and the effect

will be random. But plan ahead and you can organize formal stripes, etc. For another look, try

denim, blues, indigo, and chambray with crisp white or charcoal grays, black-and-white gingham,

spot prints, or even ticking. Or mix natural and man-made materials together—experiment! Strips of

different fabrics will, of course, be uneven to knit, so if desired, use with bulky yarns or two or more

strands of thinner yarn to give a consistent thickness. Knot the lengths together in a sequence of

texture or color, or randomly. Then start to knit. When you're finished, push all the knots through

to one side and you have a choice of using the rug rough or smooth. But whichever, you have a

beautiful texture under foot. Instead of stockinette stitch, try garter or seed stitch for extra texture.

how to make : rag rug

FOR THE RAG RUG: Use cotton fabric scraps in terry cloth, muslin, and seersucker, as well as string, cotton ribbon, and thick chenille yarn, pair size 15 knitting needles, large crochet hook

METHOD FOR THE RAG RUG: Cut the fabric scraps into strips approximately ³/₄" wide. Ply yarns together by selecting 2 or 3 strands of yarn and winding together as a ball. Now knot together various fabric strips and yarn to make a continuous length, and wind the length to create your own innovatively textured balls to knit with. Next, using size 15 needles, cast on 50 stitches. Work 1 knit row and 1 purl row alternately to form a thick stockinette-stitch fabric, using each yarn combination as it comes from the "balls." Make more "balls" as you need them.

top left: The balls of knitting "yarn" are made from a mixture of fabrics strips and thick yarns.

top center: Knot fabric strips together with multi-strands of yarn textures to make a continuous length.

top right: Add a fringe across the top and bottom of the rug.

opposite: The knots on the reverse-stockinette-stitch side of the rug create added texture.

Continue until the rug measures approximately 35¹/₂", or the desired length, from the cast-on edge. Bind off.

FINISHING: Lay the work flat and gently steam into shape. You will notice that most of the knots go to the back or "rough" side of the knitting. Either side can be used as the "right" side. For the fringe, cut strips of fabric and lengths of yarn approximately 6" long. You may find it easier to make consistent lengths by winding the yarn or fabric strips around the length of a 6" ruler and cutting through both ends. Take a single strand, fold it double, then pull the folded end through the edge of the knitting from the wrong side to the right side with a crochet hook. Slip the cut ends through the loop and pull firmly to tighten. Trim if required.

yarn : characteristics & care

CHOOSING A YARN TEXTURE: The following yarn profiles will give you an idea of some of the pros and cons of knitting with various yarn types. Remember that the secret to getting the most out of any yarn is to experiment with it, trying out various needle sizes and seeing how it looks in different stitch patterns. Also, keep in mind that the texture of the yarn alters the look of the colors it comes in. (See page 125 for details about the specific yarns used in the projects in the preceding chapters.)

Alpaca yarn: Very light and as soft and warm as cashmere, alpaca yarn is usually less expensive than cashmere. It comes in beautiful subdued natural colors. Although it can be a little prickly, it is fine to knit with.

top left: Denim yarn is machine washable and and can be tumble dried. To finish denim yarn, you first have to shrink the knitted pieces by washing them to produce the hardwearing and charateristically faded appearance (see opposite page for more about denim yarn).

top right: After washing knitted denim pieces, spin well and tumble dry. Then, if desired, air pieces for a final freshness.

Cashmere yarn: Cashmere is a noble fiber and the ultimate in luxury. It is ultra soft, light, and beautiful to the touch. One drawback of cashmere yarn is that it is expensive due to the fact that the process of producing it is costly and lengthy. Also, the knitted fabric pills easily.

Chenille yarn: With its velvet-like pile, chenille requires a little patience to knit with. One good tip is to use a size smaller needle than you think you'll need for the main knitted fabric and use a size larger to cast on with.

Cotton yarn: Cotton has a natural look and is soft and cool to the touch. It is warm in winter and cool in summer. Cotton knitting yarns come in many versions—

matte or shiny, smooth or slubby and textured. Available in a wide range of colors, it is manufactured in many thicknesses as well, from very fine to very thick. On the down side, because it has no elasticity cotton can be harder to knit than wool until you've had a little practice with it. The finished knitted fabric is often weighty and can droop easily.

Cotton and wool yarn: Mixing cotton and wool in a knitting yarn creates the ideal combination. Wool adds elasticity for ease of knitting and stretchy comfort, and cotton adds elegance to the drape of the knitted fabric and a dry, smooth coolness to the touch.

Linen yarn: Extremely dry to the touch, linen has a subtle sheen and elegant drape. Linen blended with other natural fibers is beautiful. Very resilient, most linen knitting yarns can be washed in a machine and dried in a dryer. Linen creases but this can add to its charm. Some linen can be a little harsh next to the skin.

Silk yarn: Silk has a renowned natural sheen and an exquisite drape. It is luxurious and sensuous to the touch. Although it shows off knitted details well, it is not easy to knit with since, like cotton, it has little elasticity compared to wool. Some silk yarns can pill and sag.

String: The natural texture of string has a beautiful matte surface. It is economic and easily available in various thicknesses, from fine, smooth parcel string to medium-weight general purpose string to fat, rough sisal string. It is coarse and stiff to knit and can twist during knitting, but the attractive texture makes it worthwhile.

Wool yarn: Strong and flexible, wool yarn—like cotton—is warm in winter and cool in summer. Unlike cotton, however, it can be very lofty and fine, to lofty and chunky in thickness. Wool knitting yarn comes in any number of shades and in many textures, including tweed and bouclé. The very latest wool yarn texture is the fashionably felted variety. Its elasticity makes wool easy to knit and to knit quickly into an even, regular fabric. Smooth wools like merino create very precise, elegant, and distinctive textures when knitted in raised stitch patterns, such as horizontal purl-stitch ridged stripes, vertical ribs, knit and purl checks, and fine seed stitch.

GENERAL CARE OF YARNS: The labels on most commercial yarns have instructions for washing (or dry cleaning), drying, and pressing. So for a project knitted in only one yarn, a quick look at the yarn label will tell you how to care for it. However, you may be working with several yarns in one piece, the child's blanket for example (see page 88), and in this case aftercare requires a little more thought. If one label suggests dry cleaning, then be sure to dry clean.

If in doubt about washing your knitting, it is a good idea to make a little swatch in the correct yarns and wash this to see if the fabric is effected by immersing in water or not. Watch out for shrinkage and stretching. If you are satisfied with the results, go ahead and wash by hand in warm water. Never immerse in hot water; this will "felt" your fabric for sure, and you will not be able to return it to its pre-washed state.

Natural fibers such as wool, cotton, and linen are usually best washed by hand. When hand-washing finished knitting, handle it carefully. Squeeze out excess water, never wring out. And rinse thoroughly until every particle of soap is squeezed out, as any left in will mat the fibers. Do not hang wet knitting; the weight of the water will stretch it out of shape. To dry, lay knitting out flat on top of a towel, which will absorb some of the moisture. Dry away from direct heat and leave flat until completely dry.

Check the yarn label before pressing your knitting. Most fibers only require a little steam, and the iron should be applied gently.

Look after your knits. Loose fibers can gather into balls of fluff on the surface. This is called "pilling." Cashmere and other luxury yarns are very prone to this. The fluff can be picked off or brushed over with tape.

CARE OF DENIM YARN: Denim knitting yarn is very hardwearing, practical, and machine washable. So it is great for children and adults alike. As with other indigo-dyed textiles, denim yarn will fade and age with wear and washing. Some of the dye will come off on your hands during knitting, but this washes off easily. Most of the excess dye is then lost in the initial wash. The knitted pieces will also shrink in length (but not width) during the first wash, which firms and tightens the knitting to a compact and robust fabric. This shrinkage is always allowed for in patterns that recommend denim yarn. Before you stitch knitted denim pieces together, wash them in the washing machine at 140–158°F (along with a small ball of yarn for seams). Dry the pieces flat, or tumble dry for a softer finish.

stitch gauge:tips

CHANGING THE SIZE OF YOUR KNITTING: You can change the width of your knitting to any size you want. First, knit a little bit of the proposed yarn. Then lay the knitting flat, smooth it out gently, and count how many stitches there are to 4 inches (10cm) horizontally across the stitch widths. By multiplying the number of stitches per inch (or centimeter) times the desired knitted width, you can calculate how many stitches to cast on. For example, if there are 16 stitches to 4 inches that means there are 4 per inch. So if you want a cushion 20" wide (4 x 20 = 80), then cast on 80 stitches. The number of rows per inch is usually less important, especially for simple projects—since you can just knit to the required length!

ACTUAL GAUGES FOR PROJECTS: Because the projects in this book are mostly simple cushions, throws, etc., it is usually not essential to match your stitch size exactly to the one in the original project. In other words, if your cushion or throw comes out a little bigger or smaller than the one pictured it won't matter much. If, however, you want to change the size of your knitting or match an alternative yarn to the project, the original gauge will help you with these processes, so they are given below:

PAGE 36 SIMPLE CUSHIONS: FINISHED SIZE: $19^3/_4$" (50cm) square. GAUGE FOR COTTON CUSHION: 20 stitches to 4" (10cm) over garter stitch using size 6 (4mm) needles and Rowan *Handknit D.K. Cotton.* GAUGE FOR CHENILLE CUSHION: 15 stitches to 4" (10cm) over garter stitch using size 8 (5mm) needles and Rowan *Chunky Cotton Chenille.*

PAGE 40 SEAMS CUSHION: FINISHED SIZE: 22" (55cm) square. GAUGE: 11 stitches to 4" (10cm) over stockinette stitch using size $10^1/_2$ (7mm) needles and Rowan *Chunky Soft.*

PAGE 47 STRIPE CUSHION: FINISHED SIZE: $19^3/_4$" (50cm) square. GAUGE: 15 stitches to 4" (10cm) over stockinette stitch using size 6 (4mm) needles and Rowan *Chunky Cotton Chenille.*

PAGE 52 TASSEL THROW: FINISHED SIZE: $50^1/_2$" x 44" (128cm x 111cm). GAUGE: 15 stitches and 23 rows to 4" (10cm) over stockinette stitch using size 7 ($4^1/_2$mm) needles and Rowan *Chunky Cotton Chenille.*

PAGE 56 FLOOR CUSHION: FINISHED SIZE: $28^1/_2$" (72cm) square. GAUGE: 14 stitches and 22 rows to 4" (10cm) over stockinette stitch using size 8 (5mm) needles and one strand Jaeger *Alpaca* and one strand Jaeger *Persia* together.

PAGE 61 TABLE RUNNER: FINISHED SIZE: $14^1/_2$" x 50" (37cm x 127cm). GAUGE: 12 stitches and 17 rows to 4" (10cm) over stockinette stitch using size 10 (6mm) needles and medium-weight string.

PAGE 64 BEADED CUSHIONS: FINISHED SIZE: The cushions measure $15^3/_4$" x $11^3/_4$" (40cm x 30cm). GAUGE FOR REVERSE-STOCKINETTE-STITCH CUSHION: 15 stitches to 4" (10cm) over stockinette stitch using size 7 ($4^1/_2$mm) needles and Rowan *Chunky Cotton Chenille.* "FOLD-OVER" CUSHION: 28 stitches to 4" (10cm) over stockinette stitch using size 3 ($3^1/_4$mm) needles and fingering-weight linen yarn.

PAGE 72 SQUARES THROW: FINISHED SIZE: 72" (183cm) square. GAUGE: 10 stitches to 4" (10cm) over stockinette stitch using size 11 ($7^1/_2$mm) needles and Rowan *Chunky Soft.*

PAGE 76 FELTED SWEATER: FINISHED SIZE: Finished sweater circumference is $45^1/_2$" (116cm) and finished length is 27" (68.5cm). GAUGE: $10^1/_2$ stitches and 15 rows to 4" (10cm) over stockinette stitch using size 11 ($7^1/_2$mm) needles and Rowan *Chunky Soft.*

PAGE 80 COLOR-BLOCK THROW: FINISHED SIZE: 63" (160cm) square. GAUGE FOR MERINO: 22 stitches to 4" (10cm) over stockinette stitch using size 6 (4mm) needles and Jaeger *Extra Fine Merino.* FOR PERSIA: 16 stitches to 4" (10cm) using size 7 ($4^1/_2$mm) needles and Jaeger *Persia.*

PAGE 84 BUTTON CUSHIONS: FINISHED SIZES: The cushions measure approximately $15^3/_4$" (40cm) square (not including button bands). GAUGE: 22 stitches and 32 rows to 4" (10cm) over stockinette stitch using size 6 (4mm) needles and Jaeger *Extra Fine Merino.*

PAGE 90 CHILD'S BLANKET: FINISHED SIZE: Approximately $28^1/_4$" x $35^1/_2$" (72cm x 90cm). GAUGE: 20 stitches and 28 rows to 4" (10cm) over stockinette stitch using size 5 ($3^3/_4$mm) needles and Rowan *Handknit D.K. Cotton.*

PAGE 94 CHILD'S CUSHION: FINISHED SIZE: $19^3/_4$" (50cm) square. GAUGE: 20 stitches and 28 rows before washing (20 sts and 32 rows after washing) to 4" (10cm) over stockinette stitch using size 6 (4mm) needles and Rowan *Denim.*

yarn buying:tips

PAGE 98 SIMPLE SLIPPERS: FINISHED SIZE: To fit baby, adult small, and adult medium. **GAUGE FOR D.K. COTTON:** 20 stitches and 28 rows to 10cm (4") over seed stitch using size 5 (3³/₄mm) needles and Rowan *Handknit D.K. Cotton.* **GAUGE FOR DENIM:** 20 stitches and 32 rows (before washing) to 4" (10cm) over seed stitch using size 5 (3³/₄mm) needles and Rowan *Denim.*

PAGE 105 WASH MITT: FINISHED SIZE: 7³/₄" x 6¹/₄" (20cm x 16cm). **GAUGE:** 7 stitches to 4" (10cm) over stockinette stitch using size 15 (10mm) needles and sisal string.

PAGE 108 "BAIN" BAG: FINISHED SIZE: 10¹/₂" x 11¹/₂" (27cm x 29cm). **GAUGE:** 19 stitches to 4" (10cm) over seed stitch using size 5 (3³/₄mm) needles and Rowan *Handknit D.K. Cotton.*

PAGE 112 CUDDLE COAT: FINISHED SIZE: Finished coat circumference (buttoned) is 47" (120cm) and finished length is 28" (71cm). **GAUGE:** 16 stitches and 24 rows to 4" (10cm) over stockinette stitch using size 6 (4mm) needles and Rowan *Chunky Cotton Chenille.*

PAGE 116 KNITTED BASKETS: FINISHED SIZE: Small box measures 4³/₄" x 4³/₄" x 4³/₄" (12cm x 12cm x 12cm), and large box 7" x 7" x 7" (18cm x 18cm x 18cm). **GAUGE:** 15 stitches and 25 rows to 4" (10cm) over seed stitch using size 6 (4mm) needles and medium-weight string.

PAGE 120 RAG RUG: FINISHED SIZE: Depends on rags and yarns used. **GAUGE:** Using size 15 (10mm) knitting needles, stitch and row gauge will depend on rags and yarns used.

BUYING A SUBSTITUTE YARN: If you can, it is always best to use the yarn recommended in your knitting pattern (see pages 126 and 127 for Suppliers). However, if you do decide to use an alternative yarn—in order to find a specific shade or because you can't obtain the yarn recommended—be sure to purchase a substitute yarn that is as close as possible to the original in thickness, weight, and texture so that it will be compatible with the knitting instructions. Calculate quantities required by lengths rather than by ball weights, and buy only one ball to start, so you can test the effect and the gauge.

ACTUAL YARNS USED: The following are the yarns used for the projects in the book. The descriptions will be helpful if you are trying to find an alternative yarn. **NOTE:** The *ball lengths are approximate,* and the recommended gauges are measured over stockinette stitch.

Jaeger Alpaca: 100% alpaca; a fingering-weight alpaca yarn; 201yd (184m) per 1³/₄oz (50g) ball; gauge = 28 stitches and 36 rows to 4" (10cm) using size 2–3 (3mm) needles.

Jaeger Extra Fine Merino: between a sport- and worsted-weight wool yarn; 100% extra fine merino wool; 137yd (125m) per 1³/₄oz (50g) ball; gauge = 22 stitches and 30 rows to 4" (10cm) using size 6 (4mm) needles.

Jaeger Persia: a medium-weight wool and polyamide bouclé yarn; 82% extra fine merino wool/18% polyamide; 100m (109yd) per 1³/₄oz (50g) ball; gauge = 16 stitches and 26 rows to 4" (10cm) using size 7 (4¹/₂mm) needles.

Rowan Cotton Glacé: a lightweight cotton yarn; 100% cotton; 126yd (115m) per 1³/₄oz (50g) ball; gauge = 23 stitches and 32 rows to 10cm (4") using size 3–5 (3–3³/₄mm) needles.

Rowan Chunky Cotton Chenille: a bulky-weight chenille yarn; 100% cotton; 153yd (140m) per 3¹/₂oz (100g) ball; gauge = 14–16 stitches and 23–24 rows to 4" (10cm) using size 6–8 (4–5mm) needles.

Rowan Chunky Soft: a bulky-weight felted yarn; 40% wool/30% acrylic/20% alpaca/10% polyamide, 60yd (55m) per 1³/₄oz (50g) ball; gauge – 11–12 stitches and 16 17 rows to 4" (10cm) using size 9–10¹/₂ (6¹/₂–7mm) needles.

Rowan Denim: a medium-weight cotton yarn; 100% cotton; 101yd (93m) per 1³/₄oz (50g) ball; gauge before washing = 20 stitches and 28 rows to 4" (10cm) using size 6 (4mm) needles. (See page 123 for special care instructions for denim yarn, which shrinks up to one fifth in length when first washed, but remains the same in width.)

Rowan Fine Cotton Chenille: a lightweight chenille yarn; 89% cotton/11% polyester; 175yd (160m) per 1³/₄oz (50g) ball; gauge = 20–25 stitches and 36–44 rows to 4" (10cm) using size 2–5 (2³/₄–3³/₄mm) needles.

Rowan Handknit D.K. Cotton: a medium-weight cotton yarn; 100% cotton; 92yd (85m) per 1³/₄oz (50g) ball; gauge = 19–20 stitches and 28 rows to 4" (10cm) using size 6–7 (4–4¹/₂mm) needles.

suppliers & acknowledgements

KNITTING YARNS: Full descriptions of the yarns used for the projects are given on page 125. Most of the projects in the book were worked in Rowan yarns; details for contacting Rowan Yarns and a list of selected retailers in the United States are provided below.

UNUSUAL 'YARNS' & ACCESSORIES: Other materials used for the projects, such as string, raffia, twine, beads, and buttons, are widely available in hardware stores, craft stores, and/or notions departments.

ROWAN YARNS WEBSITE
Contact the Rowan Yarns website for a complete list of retailers in the United States and for retailers in other countries.
www.rowanyarns.co.uk

ROWAN YARNS HEADQUARTERS
Rowan Yarns, Green Lane Mill, Holmfirth, West Yorkshire HD7 1RW, England. Tel: 01484 681 881

ROWAN YARNS U.S. DISTRIBUTOR
Rowan Yarns, Westminster Fibers Inc, 5 Northern Boulevard, Amherst, New Hampshire, NH 03031. Tel: (603) 886 5041/5043. Email: wfibers@aol.com

SELECTED ROWAN RETAILERS
Retailers in **bold type** are Rowan dedicated stores or departments, many offering professional help and mail-order facilities.

ALABAMA
HUNTSVILLE: Yarn Expressions, 7914 S Memorial Parkway, AL 35802. Tel (256) 881-0260

ARIZONA
TUCSON: **ROWAN AT Purls,** 7862 North Oracle Rd, AZ 85704. Tel: (520) 797-8118

CALIFORNIA
ANAHEIM HILLS: **ROWAN AT Velona Needlecraft,** 5753-B Santa Ana Canyon Rd, CA 92807. Tel: (714) 974-1570
BERKELEY: **ROWAN AT Straw Into Gold,** 3006 San Pablo Ave, CA 94702. Tel: (510) 548-5243
CARMEL: Knitting by the Sea, 5th Ave & Junipero, CA 93921. Tel: (831) 624-3189
DANVILLE: **ROWAN AT Filati Yarns,** 125 Railroad Ave, Suite F, CA 94526. Tel: (925) 820-6614
FORT BRAGG: Navarro River Knits, 301 N, Main St, CA 95437. Tel: (707) 964-9665
LOS ALTOS: **ROWAN AT Uncommon Threads,** 293 State St, CA 94022. Tel: (650) 941-1815
OAKLAND: The Knitting Basket, 2054 Mountain Blvd, CA 94611. Tel: (800) 654-4887
REDONDO BEACH: **ROWAN AT L'Atelier,** 17141/2 Catalina, CA 90277. Tel: (310) 540-4440
SAN FRANCISCO: **ROWAN AT Greenwich Yarns,** 2073 Greenwich St, CA 94123. Tel: (415) 567-2535
SAN FRANCISCO: **ROWAN AT Yarn Garden,** 545 Sutter St, Ste 202, CA 94102. Tel: (415) 956-8830
SANTA MONICA: L'Atelier on Montana, 1202 Montana Ave, CA 90403. Tel: (310) 394-4665
STUDIO CITY: La Knitterie Parisienne, 12642-44 Ventura Blvd, CA 91604. Tel: (818) 766-1515

COLORADO
COLORADO SPRINGS: Needleworks by Holly Berry, 2409 W Colorado Ave, CO 80904. Tel: (719) 636-1002
LONGMONT: Over the Moon, 600 S Airport Rd, Bldg A, Ste D, CO 80503. Tel: (303) 485-6778

CONNECTICUT
WESTPORT: **ROWAN AT Hook 'N' Needle,** 1869 Post Rd East, CT 06880. Tel: (203) 259-5119

ILLINOIS
CHICAGO: Barkim Ltd, 47 W Polk St, IL 60605. Tel: (888) 548-2211. Mail order only. Email: BarkimLtd@aol.com
CHICAGO: Weaving Workshop, 2218 N Lincoln Ave, IL 60614. Tel: (773) 929-5776
CLARENDON HILLS: Flying Colors Inc, 154 Burlington, IL 60514. Tel: (630) 325-0888
EVANSTON: Closeknit Inc, 622 Grove St, IL 60201. Tel: (847) 328 6760
ST CHARLES: The Fine Line Creative Arts Center, 6 N 158 Crane Rd, IL 60175. Tel: (630) 584-9443

INDIANA
FT WAYNE: Cass Street Depot, 1044 Cass St, IN 46802. Tel: (219) 20-2277
INDIANAPOLIS: Mass Avenue Knit Shop, 521 East North St, IN 46204. Tel: (800) 675-8565

KENTUCKY
LOUISVILLE: Handknitters Limited, 11705 Main St, KY 40243. Tel: (502) 254-9276

KANSAS
LAWRENCE: **ROWAN AT The Yarn Barn,** 930 Mass Ave, KS 66044. Tel: (800) 468-0035

MAINE
CAMDEN: Stitchery Square, 11 Elm St, ME 04843. Tel: (207) 236-9773
FREEPORT: **ROWAN AT Grace Robinson & Co,** 475 US Rte 1, Ste 1, ME 04032. Tel: (207) 865-6110

MARYLAND
BALTIMORE: **ROWAN AT Woolworks,** 6305 Falls Rd, MD 21209. Tel: (410) 337-9030
BETHESDA: **ROWAN AT Needlework Attic,** 4706 Bethseda Ave, MD 20814. Tel: (800) 654-6654
BETHESDA: **ROWAN AT Yarns International,** 5110 Ridgefield Rd, MD 20816. Tel: (301) 913-2980

GLYNDON: Woolstock, 4848 Butler Rd, MD 21701. Tel: (410) 517-1020

MASSACHUSETTS
CAMBRIDGE: Woolcott & Co, 61 JFK St, MA 02138-4931. Tel: (617) 547-2837
HARVARD: The Fiber Loft, Rt 111, PO Building, MA 01451. Tel: (800) 874-9276
LEXINGTON: **ROWAN AT Wild & Woolly Studio,** 7A Meriam St, MA 02173. Tel: (781) 861-7717
LENOX: **ROWAN AT Colorful Stitches,** 48 Main St, MA 01240. Tel: (800) 413-6111

MICHIGAN
BIRMINGHAM: Knitting Room, 251 Merrill, MI 48009. Tel: (248) 540-3623
HOWELL: A Stitch in Time, 722 East Grand River, MI 48843. Tel: (517) 546-0769
TAWAS BAY: Tawas Bay Yarn Co., 402 W Lake St, MI 48763. Tel: (517) 362-4463
TRAVERSE CITY: Lost Art Yarn Shoppe, 123 East Front St, MI 49684. Tel (616) 941-1263
WYOMING: Threadbender Yarn Shop, 2767 44th St, SW, MI 49509. Tel: (888) 531-6642

MINNESOTA
MINNEAPOLIS: **ROWAN AT Linden Hills Yarn,** 2720 W 3rd St, MN 55410. Tel: (612) 929-1255
MINNETONKA: Skeins 11309 Highway 7, MN 55305. Tel (612) 939-4166
ST PAUL: **ROWAN AT The Yarnery KMK Crafts,** 840 Grand Ave, MN 55105. Tel: (651) 222 5793
WHITE BEAR LAKE: **ROWAN AT A Sheepy Yarn Shoppe,** 2185 Third St, MN 55110. Tel: (800) 480-5462

MONTANA
STEVENSVILLE: Wild West Wools, 3920 Suite B Highway 93N, MO 59870. Tel: (406) 777-4114

NEBRASKA

OMAHA: **ROWAN AT Personal Threads Boutique,** 8025 W Dodge Rd, NB 68114. Tel: (402) 391-7733

NEW HAMPSHIRE

CENTER HARBOR: Keepsake Yarnworks, Senter's Market, Rt 25, NH 03226. Tel: (800) 865-9458

CONCORD: Elegant Ewe, 71 S Main St, NH 03301. Tel: (603) 226-0066

EXETER: Charlotte's Web, Exeter Village Shops, 137 Epping Rd, Rt 27, NH 03833. Tel: (888) 244-6460

NEW JERSEY

CHATHAM: Stitching Bee, 240A Main St, NJ 07928. Tel: (973) 635-6691

GARWOOD: Knitter's Workshop Inc, 345 North Ave, NJ 07027. Tel: (908)789-1333

LAMBERTVILLE: Simply Knits, 23 Church St, NJ 08530. Tel: (609) 397-7101

SPARTA: Yarn Loft, 580 Rt 15, NJ 07871. Tel: (973) 383-6667

NEW MEXICO

ALBUQUERQUE: Village Wools, 3801 San Mateo Ave, NE, NM 87110. Tel: (505) 883-2919

SANTA FE: Needle's Eye, 927 Paseo de Peralta, NM 87501. Tel: (505) 982-0706

NEW YORK

BEDFORD HILLS: Lee's Yarn Center, 733 N Bedford Rd, NY 10507. Tel: (914) 244-3400

Brooklyn: Heartmade (Mail Order only), 877 East 10th St, 2nd Floor, NY 11230. Tel: (800) 898-4290

BUFFALO: Elmwood Yarn Shop, 1639 Hertel Ave, NY 14216. Tel: (716) 834 7580

GARDEN CITY: **ROWAN AT Garden City Stitches,** 725 Franklin Ave, NY 11530. Tel: (516) 739-5648

HUNTINGTON: Knitting Corner, 718 New York Ave, NY 11743. Tel: (516) 421-2660

ITHACA: The Homespun Boutique, 314 E State Street, NY 14850. Tel: (607) 277-0954

NEW YORK CITY: The Yarn Company, 2274 Broadway, NY 10024. Tel: (212) 787-7878

NEW YORK CITY: **ROWAN AT Yarn Connection,** 218 Madison Ave, NY 10016. Tel: (212) 684-5099

SKANEATELES: **ROWAN AT Elegant Needles,** 5 Jordan St, NY 13152. Tel: (315) 685-9276

OHIO

AURORA: Edie's Knit Shop, 214 Chillicothe Rd, OH 44202 Tel: (330) 562-7226

CINCINNATI: **ROWAN AT Wizard Weavers,** 2701 Observatory Rd, OH 45208. Tel: (513) 871-5750

CLEVELAND: Fine Points, 2026 Murray Hill, OH 44106. Tel: (216) 229-6644

COLUMBUS: Wolfe Fiber Arts, 1188 W 5th Ave, OH 43212. Tel: (614) 487-9980

OREGON

ASHLAND: Web-sters, 11 North Main St, OR 97520. Tel: (800) 482-9801

COOS BAY: My Yarn Shop, 264 B Broadway, OR 97420. Tel: (541) 266-8230

EUGENE: Northwest Peddlers, 2101 Bailey Hill Rd S, OR 97402. Tel: (541) 65-9003

EUGENE: Soft Horizons, 412 East 13th Ave, OR 97401. Tel: (541) 343-0651

LAKE OSWEGO: Molehill Farm, 16722 SW Boones Ferry Rd, OR 97035. Tel: (503) 697-9554

PENNSYLVANIA

KENNETT SQUARE: Wool Gathering, 131 East State St, PA 19348. Tel: (610) 444-8236

PHILADELPHIA: **ROWAN AT Sophie's Yarns,** 2017 Locust St, PA 19103. Tel: (215) 977-9276

PHILADELPHIA: Tangled Web, 7900 Germantown Ave, PA 19118. Tel: (215) 242-1271

SEWICKLEY: Yarns Unlimited, 435 Beaver St, PA 15143. Tel: (412) 741-8894

RHODE ISLAND

PROVIDENCE: **ROWAN AT A Stitch Above Ltd,** 190 Wayland Ave, RI 02906. Tel: (800) 949-5648

TIVERTON: **ROWAN AT Sakonnet Purls,** 3988 Main Rd, RI 02878. Tel: (888) 624-9902

TENNESSEE

KINGSPORT: The Needlecraft Inc, 201 Colonial Heights Rd, TN 37663 Tel: (423) 239-5791

TEXAS

SAN ANTONIO: The Yarn Barn of San Antonio, 4300 McCullough, 78212. Tel: (210) 826-3679

VERMONT

WOODSTOCK: **ROWAN AT The Whippletree,** 7 Central St, VT 05091. Tel: (802) 457-1325

VIRGINIA

CHARLOTTESVILLE: It's A Stitch Inc, 188 Zan Rd, VA 22901. Tel: (804) 973-0331

FALLS CHURCH: Aylin's Woolgatherer, 7245 Arlington Blvd. #318, VA 22042. Tel: (703) 573-1900

MCLEAN: **ROWAN AT Wooly Knits,** 6728 Lowell Ave, VA 22101. Tel: (800) 767-4036

MIDDLEBURG: Hunt Country Yarns, 1 West Federal St, VA 20118-1206. Tel: (540) 687 5129

Richmond: The Knitting Basket, 5812 Grove Ave, VA 23226. Tel: (804) 282-2909

RICHMOND: Got Yarn, 8200 Buford Oaks Rd, VA 23235. Tel: (804) 272-1117. Mail order and internet orders only. Email: 2savages@home.com

WASHINGTON

BELLEVUE: Parkside Wool Company, 17 102nd Ave, NE, WA 98004. Tel: (425) 455-2138

OLYMPIA: Canvas Works, 317 N Capitol, WA 98501. Tel: (360) 352-4481

POULSBO: Lauren's Wild & Wooly, 19020 Front St, WA 98370. Tel: (360) 779-3222

SEATTLE: **ROWAN AT The Weaving Works,** 4717 Brooklyn Ave, NE, WA 98105. Tel: (888) 524-1221

WISCONSIN

APPLETON: Jane's Knitting Hutch, 132 E. Wisconsin Ave, WI 54911. Tel: (920) 954 9001

DELEVAN: Studio S Fiber Arts, W8903 County Hwy A, WI 53115. Tel: (608) 883-2123

ELM GROVE: The Yarn House, 940 Elm Grove Rd, WI 53122. Tel: (414) 786-5660

MADISON: The Knitting Tree Inc, 2614 Monroe St, WI 53711. Tel: (608) 238-0121

MILWAUKEE: Ruhama's, 420 E Silver Spring Dr, WI 53217. Tel: (414) 332-2660

WAUSAU: The Black Purl, 300 Third St, WI 54403. Tel: (715) 843-7875

AUTHOR'S ACKNOWLEDGEMENTS

To a very special team of people, who have each contributed a unique skill, and for their creative spirit, inspiration, dedication, patience, enthusiasm, endless support and that special artistic 'eye'.

With warmest thanks to **Kate Kirby, Susan Berry, Debbie Mole, John Heseltine, Stephen Sheard, Sally Harding, Sarah Phillips, Sally Lee, Hannah Davis, Wendy, Lyndsay** and **Kim at Rowan,** and **my daughter Bella** for, well, just about everything!

And a heartfelt thank you to all those anonymous women who have knitted, stitched and created, whose work I have discovered in flea markets and jumble sales all over the world and whose love and soul were stitched and worked into every fibre. Many of these women had no formal outlet for their work, just passion for their crafts. They continue to be a constant source of ideas and inspiration.

index